FORGIVEN MUCH
TO LOVE MUCH

Guardian BOOKS

Belleville, Ontario, Canada

FORGIVEN MUCH—TO LOVE MUCH
Copyright © 2003, Jane Page

All Scripture quotations, unless otherwise specified, are from *The Holy Bible, King James Version.* Copyright © 1977, 1984, Thomas Nelson Inc., Publishers.

National Library of Canada Cataloguing in Publication
Page, Jane, 1914-
    Forgiven much, to love much / Jane Page.
ISBN 1-55306-563-8.—ISBN 1-55306-565-4 (LSI ed.)

    1. Page, Jane, 1914- 2. Christian biography—United States.
I. Title.
BR1725 P22 A3 2003   277.3'082'092   C2003-901192-5

**For more information or
to order additional copies, please contact:**

Jane Page
P.O. Box 546
Edneyville NC 28727
USA

Guardian Books is an imprint of *Essence Publishing,* a Christian Book Publisher dedicated to furthering the work of Christ through the written word. For more information, contact:

20 Hanna Court, Belleville, Ontario, Canada K8P 5J2
Phone: 1-800-238-6376 • Fax: (613) 962-3055
E-mail: publishing@essencegroup.com
Internet: www.essencegroup.com

Printed in Canada
by

*The cover design depicts my painting of the colorful brick wall
viewed from the window of my rented room in Detroit,
as described in chapter thirteen.*

*I wish to express thanks and gratitude for the many friends
who encouraged me, by their support in many ways,
thus helping to make possible the numerous labors
incident to producing this book.*

May the Lord reward their kindness.

Introduction

This story of my life is told according to the leading and ability God has given me. In common with all biographies, some mundane incidents are included that led to the development of circumstances, events, attitudes and decisions of consequence. I trust that this account of my life and conversion to Christ will merit your interest, of course, but more than that—I pray it will propel the reader toward spiritual insights regarding the way God works to bring souls unto Himself. It is for this purpose that our joy is fulfilled.

Since I have no wish to magnify sin with detailed descriptions of wrong and evil conduct, my story will not pander to base curiosity about acts of sin and degradation. I could be accused of being ashamed of the sin in my life. You would be right. I would be ashamed of *not* being ashamed. I believe I have told enough to identify myself as a sinner. The depth to which I confess is contrasted to the glorious heights to which the Lord has lifted me.

As to my beginning walk with God, there is no concealment. I have bared my soul—revealing my weak and faltering first steps. I speak not from a pinnacle of strength, but from a valley of weakness from which the Lord is ever leading me to higher ground.

Christian biographies I have read were written about believers of some fame in their ministry and of laudable reputations for faith and wisdom. One gets the impression of flawlessness since the day of their conversions. It is different with me. As you read about my life, you are not sitting at the feet of one towering above average believers. You are sitting with one whose flesh is as weak as your own. You are reading of one in whom the Lord has begun a good work, which He will continue until this poor earthen vessel is at last presented, faultless, before the Father.

I feel I must let the reader know how far in time I am now from the events I've related. Back then, bread could be bought for five cents a loaf, and ten cents was the price of a hamburger. From the time of my birth in 1914 to the time I was converted to Christ in 1940, the cost of a postage stamp increased from two to three cents, which was considered inflationary. My room rent was $4.00 a week. You have an idea of the time covered in my story by my disclosure of the date of my birth. A little simple arithmetic will show you how old I am now.

Clarifying the time frame might make for better visual pictures of dress fashions, car styles, and technologies of the time, but the heart and focus of what I am wanting to tell is how the Lord Jesus changed my life and saved my soul, and the lives and souls of others. My theme is God's gracious salvation—above and beyond the confines of time. I should at this point tell you that my two dear friends who, upon their conversion to Christ, labored with me in the Lord's work (Maude Oberg and Clara De Runts), are now "at home with the Lord"—and thus, the three-fold cord is temporarily broken until the Day the cord is united and divinely woven with countless other cords, bound together for all eternity.

To me and to many who have heard my testimony, the story of my conversion to Christ transcends the human excitement that pales as emotions soar to the dimension of thrilled hearts and blessed souls. I am speaking not of what I have done, but what my merciful Savior has done for me.

Perhaps I should be skillful enough to let the reader figure out "the bottom line"—the sum of what I am saying. But I can't keep still. I'll do the very emotional, unprofessional, common thing and shout in print: "WHAT MY LORD HAS DONE FOR ME, HE WILL DO FOR YOU!"—Will you believe it? When you do, you too, will want to shout, "I know! I know I'm saved!" You may be one who has already believed and joyfully shouted. Whether you shout or not, the music of heaven will vibrate in your soul forevermore. Hallelujah! What a Savior!

Jane Page

PART ONE

Chapter One

The gray dawn was striped with heavy black lines as I saw it from the barred window of the State Hospital in Kankakee, Illinois. A young woman of twenty-six, my outlook was as bleak as my tear-blurred vision of the dismal surroundings. "Why am I here?" I asked rebelliously. I was not wondering, really, for I knew very well why they committed me from the psychopathic ward of the County Hospital in Chicago to this place (alcohol abuse).

In bitter spirit, I sat sullenly holding onto the bars—tangible restraints to my freedom. Outside, the neatly landscaped grounds stretched their spacious green carpet—a view as frustrating as a mirage to a wayfarer of the desert. My barren desert was the drab interior of this vault, in which I was securely locked to sit dejectedly, day after day, regretting the past and dreading the future.

Patients on the ward shuffled about like uncanny specters. Watching them through weeks of dreary days, I had come to think of them as the walking dead. Faces were like those you saw when you bent over coffins—cold, immobile, expressionless—except for the eyes!

Eyes were open; staring, unseeing, tragic eyes that made me turn away, fearing to probe their depth. Shoulders slumped; arms hung as loose pendulums, without gesture and without grace. Dull faded clothing clad hollow chests with drooping breasts. The whole ward was a forest of scrawny human frames with shapeless, bony limbs. I thought of Kipling's "rag and a bone and a hank of hair."

This was one of the admitting wards where patients were observed and classified before their assignment to permanent or "home" wards. Female patients with various types of mental illness were regimented to a mild and obedient behavior. Those who could not be controlled were immediately sent to wards for disturbed patients, where restraints and hydrotherapy were used. From the patient's viewpoint, "hydro" (where they were wrapped in cold wet sheets) was a punishment for disorderly conduct or any opposition to authority.

From the day I arrived, I had scanned searchingly for eyes that were something more than burnt holes, and found a few with the spark I hoped for. These were patients who still had their mental faculties (alcoholics, drug addicts, attempted suicides). These patients I could at least talk to, and although I was never gregarious by nature, I did find a certain camaraderie—a peculiar kinship in misery.

It was indeed a strange place in which to seek social status, but there were a few patients who strutted in self-styled sophistication and considered themselves the elite of "inmate-land." I aspired to be among them, and it was with real effort that I masked my despondency and grief with a smirk and paid homage to toilet-room wit with feigned laughter. I managed to contribute my share of brusque humor, for I had adopted the life habit of assuming the role of skeptic, perversely enjoying the reputation without ever having felt the unalloyed cynicism I pretended. Ashamed that I did not actually feel amused contempt for decency and conventional morality that smart people felt, I pretended a contempt I didn't feel.

Conversations flipped like a tossed coin. There were only two sides, of course. Alternately, we condemned and cursed the circumstances and powers we thought responsible for our plight, then turned to bragging about our past—grossly exaggerating exploits and professing a former state of glamour and prosperity. Each pretended to believe the other's lies. We did that—and we played cards. To add zest to our game, we made bets. Gambling among patients was strictly forbidden, but we were not of a citizenry who obeyed rules gladly. Our card playing was apparent to the attendants and others—an approved pastime for patients by default. No one ever reported us.

I had a knack for losing. My cigarettes went. I had been allowed to carry some change on my person. I lost that, too. I wanted to stay in the game, and so I put in a request for some money that was held in trust for me at the hospital's administration building. It was the money I had with me when I was committed. Patients' requests for a dollar or two from their trust funds were usually granted, for there was a commissary on the grounds where such things as candy bars and cigarettes could be purchased. But I asked for ten dollars. That was a mistake. The sum was objectionable, much more than I could possibly need in view of the trivial purchases available to patients. Patients were not permitted to draw in excess of needs for a week. I found myself being interrogated. Why did I need that much? Not daring to confess to gambling, I lied: "I need the money for cigarettes."

I was on a restricted ward. Patients were free to smoke only at intervals when attendants opened the door to empty garbage. Attendants stood with us outside by the garbage pails while those of us who smoked finished a cigarette. This was usually right after mealtimes. At best, under such arrangements, I could smoke only three or four cigarettes a day. The doctor in charge of the ward knew there was something amiss, but she must have known also that questioning me would not unearth the truth. She did not press beyond the cigarette alibi. Her sharp eyes flashed as she accused, "You alcoholics think this is a rest home, don't you? Well, I'll put you where you really can smoke ten dollars worth of cigarettes if you want to." (At fifteen cents a pack back in 1939, that would be about 100 packs.) I was not delighted, for I was aware that the promised privilege held with it some dark threat.

I soon learned what the doctor had meant. There were a hundred and fifty patients on Ward 8-North where she was planning to put me. There were alcoholics and drug addicts of a tougher fiber, but most of the patients were psychotic, having frequent seizures of temper known and charted by attendants as "disturbed spells." I dreaded and feared this ward, which was noted for outbreaks of violence. I had heard of how Dr. Morrow, the Superintendent, lost his eye when a patient, during a "disturbed spell," attacked him while he was passing through one of the north wards.

On Ward 8-North, the patients were crowded together in one huge room that lacked enough chairs or benches for everybody to sit on. Upstairs in the ward's dormitory, the narrow cots were so close together patients had to sidle between them. However, the building had a wire-screened porch—patients who smoked could get a light from an attendant and go out on the porch and smoke as often as they wished. The doctor had not lied.

A tremor of terror seized me. Like one struggling in the dark, I struck out in every direction against imaginary foes. My fight was not physical, of course. In such a place as this, specters haunted sick, tormented minds every day—specters that would never come into being. My specters—dreads and fears which my mind readily conceived—could certainly materialize, for danger on such a ward as 8-North was not impossible, indeed, it was most probable.

I knew that if I pleaded my fears to attendants, they would only make note that I was "distressed" (a point not in my favor). Even in the event that one could be found who would sympathize, she would be helpless in preventing this transfer. Doctor Weaver, whose prejudice against cigarette-smoking alcoholics had goaded her into planning my transfer, would no doubt refuse my request to talk with her again. And if she did see me and listen, the fact that I disliked and feared association with the patients of 8-North would not soften her heart, I knew. She would in all probability bristle at the implied criticism of the ward's unsafe condition.

I had one ray of hope—a very faint glimmer, but I fanned it to a bright enthusiasm. Parents of patients could sometimes help in some situations. I would try to persuade my father to do something about this. I would beg him.

Chapter Two

My father? Was he always kind to me? I'm sure he never intended to be otherwise, but even I could see that his leniency did not produce the good fruits his heart desired for me. Would he listen now that I needed him so much? He might not understand and could refuse to cooperate, no matter how frantically I begged. Both hope and fear lodged conflictingly in my heart.

Now retired on old age pension, my father had been a hard-working sign painter who hated his business because it meant he had failed as an artist. He had real ability in art, but because there was some lack in him, he dissipated his youth to the neglect of his talent and sober responsibilities. William Page married young and soon deserted his wife, and roamed with the Bohemian clan that seemed to intrigue him. He let his wife obtain a divorce, accepting his "freedom" without protest. It was in an effort toward self-reform that he finally quit his crowd and started to paint signs for a living.

He met Nettie Walley, who ran a rooming house where he rented, and soon proposed marriage to the beautiful young widow. He pledged to love and provide for her and her young son, Raymond. Despite misgivings instilled by her puritanical upbringing, Nettie married William Page, telling herself she would surely convert him from his atheistic views which he flaunted quite openly.

Things just did not work out. A year after their marriage, these two people knew that whatever had drawn them together was forever gone. There were criticisms. While Billy Page found fault with Raymond, Nettie came to see that much was wrong with her new husband. Their views were aired, and thus the walls of their habitation echoed with lamentations. They no longer cared for each other and both agreed to no longer share the marriage bed.

It was a decision made too late for complete comfort, for I was already on the way. Mother frankly told my father she did not want his child. A living child could be the fetter that chains a man to a long, loveless union from which he would otherwise be free—unless, of course, he deserted this wife as he did the wife of his youth. But he had long suffered scathing self-reproach for his desertion of his first wife. He decided that were a child born, he would have to stick this time. But he, too, had no desire for a child from this marriage.

In the city of Chicago, in the first week of July 1914, the doctor assured my mother before he left the city on vacation that her baby wasn't due for another two weeks. Contrary to the doctor's predictions, however, and contrary to the desires and hopes of my parents, I nevertheless arrived. I was born in a back room of my father's sign shop on 31st Street in Chicago—my parents' living quarters. Early in the morning of July 8th, Father heard Mother's groans. In the agony of childbirth, she told him, "You will have to bring this baby into the world." There was no time to scrub the paint stains from his hands. In throes of pain, Mother managed to instruct him through the delivery. I do not remember, of course, my first upside-down view of this confusing old world as I dangled from my father's grasp. But my tiny presence broke upon the awareness of my parents through their sense of hearing. (My squeals, naturally).

In the days that followed, the doctor's diagnosis and prognosis offered them hope for a way out—freedom from the one link chaining them to matrimony. My death was predicted. My parents had long ceased to be lovers, but Father reached for Mother's hand. They searched each other's eyes and both were glad as Mother voiced their decision: "We will do everything we can to save her life." She felt his grasp on her hand tighten.

My parents fought for my life. Mother worked devotedly, frantically, unceasingly—massaging, bathing, caressing—to defeat the progression of the ailment, which was rickets. When at last it looked as though I would pull through, the doctor marveled. "Mrs. Page," he said, "No greater nursing have I ever witnessed. You are to be praised." Mother acknowledged, "Yes, I worked, but God gave His guidance and blessing because God Himself wants this child to live."

I, a being whose first living breath was unwelcome to those whom nature decreed should rejoice, eventually found a niche in existence and a place in two human hearts. My father filled his days delighting in his new baby. He cradled me in his arms, walking the floor and humming. For hours he would sit holding me in his lap. As I grew older he still doted on me, and any toy my heart desired was not withheld. Mother would remonstrate. "It isn't good for her to always get everything she wants. When she grows up, she will be shocked to discover that life isn't like that." But his philosophy was, "They are only kids once."

Mother's manner was always gentle and her voice was soft as a melody. I loved her. One day she drew me to her. "Long ago, dear, when people did bad things, they had to sacrifice animals. Innocent little sheep and other creatures died for people's sins. Then Jesus came and they nailed Him to a cross. He died for the sins of all." To Mother, it was a solemn moment. Her child was hearing about Jesus for the first time. She waited, hoping for some word or manner that would indicate this story had moved me. She saw only my look of puzzlement. I asked one question, "After Jesus died, did they still kill the poor animals?" Her voice remained soft, unhurried.

"No, after Jesus died, the sin debt was forever paid and no animal had to die to atone for sin." I smiled much too brightly. "I'm glad," I said, "I'm glad about the animals." This was not at all satisfactory. An urgency entered her tone as Mother pressed, "But don't you see? Jesus died to save people like you and me!" I turned my head from side to side negatively. "No, He died to save the animals."

In heat of spirit, Mother told me she wanted me to be a good Christian like my brother Raymond. She said that she and her first husband had a little girl, Marion, who had died and was in heaven now. Raymond and Marion had accepted the wonderful story of the Savior's sacrifice. Why couldn't I? I was interested and asked many questions about Marion. What was she like? What was the color of her hair? Her eyes? Mother described her as a tender, beautiful, angelic child. I was enthralled with the story of a sister so lovely in heaven. "Mother," I asked, "Am I anything like her?" I do not remember whether she replied immediately or if her answer came slowly after a pause given to thought. I don't even remember the words she spoke. I know only that their meaning gave me pain. In spite of tender years, I could discern a limitation being placed upon me. Was I never to hope to be among the best?

My dear mother could not have known, of course, that my child's heart was swelling with a new sad feeling for Jesus, because He had died to save those animals. I had not yet learned to love human beings, but I easily adored furry dumb creatures with their nervous tender noses and their sad soulful eyes, and I loved Jesus for what He did for them. It was a beginning—but the new warm feeling was being chilled by the confusing inadequacy in myself of which I had just been made aware. I seemed to read a meaning—perhaps beyond her meaning—in the words she said, which I didn't understand and couldn't remember. She had hugged me to her, but it was a hug more desperate than loving, and I sensed this.

I was not old enough to read when my father called me to him one day. He cupped my face in his big hands and said, "Dear child, promise Daddy you will never believe the Bible." I did not know what he was talking about, but it seemed that a shroud of painful sadness settled over me. I quickly promised, "I won't believe it, Daddy."

My parents seemed to disagree on almost everything, and of course, they could not agree on training me. Mother wanted to choose my companions. If the children of the neighborhood (which was fast deteriorating) were of a caliber unrefined and lacking in mannerly conduct, she would much rather that I remain alone and play by myself. Her scrutiny was very keen, and I found myself alone much of the time. My father would storm, "There are no bad kids. Adults can turn out bad, but children are all innocent. No harm can possibly come from her playing with any child, no matter what the background." Thus he tried to overrule Mother's objections. In some battles he was the victor, but in others, as this one, my mother triumphed.

When I was still very young, we moved to Indiana Avenue and 31st Street in Chicago. There was a large courtyard in the back of the building where I could play. It was all cemented; there was no grass at all, and ball playing was prohibited because of the apartment house windows all around. However, children have ways of amusing themselves, and I managed to find enjoyment although I longed for other children to play with.

One day, some boys came into the courtyard. They were a bit older and very pleasant, and they asked if I always played only in the one place. I told them that I did. Then they invited me to join them in a vacant lot across the street. They had potatoes and wieners, which they roasted over an open fire. When I asked where they got them, they laughed and said they had "hooked " them. I didn't know what that meant. But the boys were wonderful, I thought, and when I learned they were all members of a gang, I asked if I might join. I found that all seven of them were captains—first captain, second, third, and fourth, etc.—

their rank determined by their pugilistic abilities. The first captain was first captain because he could lick every member of the gang. The second captain could beat up every member except the first captain, and so on down the line. If I wanted to join, I could, but I would have to take my place as eighth captain unless I wanted to fight my way to higher rank. Someone suggested I fight the seventh captain if I didn't want to take the lowest place. To that I objected, "No, I'd rather be third captain. I'll fight with him."

The third captain was a very dark, wiry little fellow with a toothless grin. He doubled up his fists and pranced around in eagerness to defend his title. I removed my sweater and pitched in, hitting and punching. I did not pull hair. That would be poor sportsmanship, I thought.

To this day, I think the leader shot a glance at the third captain that told him to lose, for I was quickly proclaimed champion and awarded a badge—a square of cardboard with "No. 3" penciled on it—and praised with much gusto. Even my defeated opponent was taking it joyously. My pride and joy were boundless.

Home with my mother, thoughts were racing happily on the details of my victory, and I could not hold them in check long enough to pursue the dull business of analyzing how my mother would take all this. I rushed in, "Mother, I'm third captain!" Mm-hmm," she said, perhaps wondering if my teddy bear and doll were the first and second captains. Failing to impress her, I said, "It's for real, Mother. I'm third captain of a real live gang."

Something about the word "gang" snapped her to attention. "What did you say? Did you say you belong to a *gang*?" I nodded proudly. Then Mother went into a lecture on gangs—how objectionable they were and certainly not the thing for nice little girls. I felt my hard-won membership slipping through my fingers and tried to think of some convincing argument, but I couldn't.

Mother concluded, "Now dear, you tell those little girls who have the poor taste to call themselves a gang that your mother will not permit you to remain a member."

"But Mother, they are not girls. They are a gang of boys. I got my place as third captain because I could fight better than all the other captains except the first and second ones." Mother turned off the gas on the cookstove and sat down. "My young daughter with a gang of boys!" she moaned. "How awful! This is simply terrible!"

"But these are nice boys," I protested, eager to set my mother right. "These boys are swell kids!"

That did it. I was not allowed out alone to play for days after that. My father threw his head back and laughed as Mother recounted this tale. He was not horrified as she was, but he did agree that I should not see the boys again.

He felt sorry for me, though, and thinking to add zest to my lonely life, he proposed, "Jane, you go to the bakery around the corner and buy a lemon pie for tonight, will you?"

I was delighted with the importance of being asked to do this shopping errand. I was quite old enough, but it was the first time my folks had ever sent me to the store. Even my father was overly protective and had forbidden me to cross a street. The nearby bakery could be reached without encountering such a hazard. The act of purchasing was simple enough and the glory of the moment soon forgotten, but when at the table my father feigned enthusiasm, I was much impressed and became very proud when he said, "This is the best pie I ever ate in my whole life. Jane, you are the best pie buyer in the world." That was nice to hear. Very nice. My father was lavish in his praise. I did not discern that it was overdone—a product of his sympathy for my loneliness. I wanted more praise and I thought I knew how to get it.

Shortly after that event, Father got a telephone call from Mrs. Moyer, the bakery woman. She asked, "Mr. Page, do you want ten dollars worth of pies?"

What would ever make her think such a thing, my father wondered. He soon found out. He was told his little daughter was at that moment standing in the bakery shop waiting to be given ten dollars worth of pies that she had just ordered. Thus his praise of my purchasing ability came to an abrupt end.

I was not a healthy child. In quick succession, and for long, drawn-out periods of time, I had chicken pox, mumps, measles, scarlet fever, small pox, and pneumonia. Some of these illnesses were "close calls," but Mother's skillful and devoted nursing always brought me through. She was careful to point out that it was only because God blessed her efforts. Being sick so much of the time, I missed kindergarten and the lower grades of school. But I did not miss out on the knowledge to be gained during those years—my mother had been a schoolteacher, and she taught me. When finally my siege of illness passed, I was able to enter a higher grade than most children of my age. I became a "little-un" among much older children in the racially integrated school of my district in Chicago.

With a natural shyness born of playing alone so much, I did not fit in very well with the others. There was a certain excitement in their natures that I did not have. At recess, when boys and girls rushed from classrooms screaming in delight, I found no such glee bubbling within me. Although I would have enjoyed the slides, swings and teeter-totters, that playground area was crowded with rowdy, happy, lively children and I shrank from them. I feared the shoving and mauling I would surely encounter in the process of waiting my turn for a chance to slide or swing. Usually, there was no waiting turn. Kids scrambled and butted each other in their efforts to be "next." But once in a while, by someone's ability to shout louder than the prevailing din of shrill voices, a sensible suggestion to "stand in line" was adhered to.

On one such occasion, I deserted my post of isolation and stepped to the end of a line forming for the toboggan slide. Other children were lining up in back of me. The one in front jiggled in anxious impatience, while the girl in back was pushing. I wanted to step out and run back to my wall, but I dreaded the attention my retreat would surely bring. I was terribly self-conscious, so I stuck it out. At least I was trying to, when the school "bully," by the name of Jessie (yes, "bully" among girls), decided she wanted my place. She simply tapped me on the shoulder, saying, "Get to the back of the line. I'm taking your place." I started to answer but my voice wouldn't sound. Impatiently, "Go to the back!" Jessie ordered.

That night in bed, I shifted the pillow restlessly. My tears had made it wet. Shame and frustration were eating at me. Why had I obeyed Jessie? Why had I said nothing and let that girl take my turn on the slide? I knew why. I was afraid Jessie would beat me. Fearing a beating was fearing the unknown, really. My parents had always disciplined me with words only. I had never suffered any type of corporal punishment. I did not really know what a beating felt like. Still, I was afraid. I was afraid to even talk to the other girls in my class. I didn't have a shrill little voice like the rest of them. Mine was deep and a little hoarse. I was ashamed of my voice. I had never felt ashamed of it at home, had never even been conscious of its low-pitched quality. But at school when I was called upon to recite, the other children would laugh and some would thrust out their lips and grunt from their stomachs, making a mock of my tones. It embarrassed me and made me unhappy in school. I found solace in deep concentration in my lessons. And of course, I was made fun of for that. The teacher, perhaps aware of the situation and seeking to come to my rescue, would praise my ability to learn and my good behavior. But that certainly failed to endear me to the others, for after all, I was the youngest in the class.

My self-loathing came to a climax one day when, in the vacant lot across from the school, a dray horse that had been hit by a car lay dying. The man standing by had sent someone to get a policeman to shoot it. A swarm of kids looked on. My curiosity drove me to look, too. It was the first time I had seen any creature die. The horse was on its side, its flanks wet with a pungent-smelling sweat and its abdomen heaving heavily. The animal's eyes were wide open and had a glassy look. The nostrils were dilated and a white foam frothed from the mouth. I indulged in deep draughts of looking—and then I was shaken from my fixed stare by tittering sounds.

My first thought was of myself. Were they laughing at me? Had I been looking too intensely? But no! They were unconscious of my presence. The children were giggling and tittering at the horse's suffering. One child rolled his eyes and threw back his head, imitating labored breathing. "I'm dying! I'm dying!" he squealed. The laughter increased. One pointed to the foam around the horse's mouth. "Look, he's blowing bubbles!" That brought a howl. The animal's strong legs were twitching. I hadn't noticed that. Someone screamed, in jolly delight, "Look, he thinks he's running!" The laughter was a loud roar. I looked about and saw everybody laughing. I felt different again—ashamed that I was not able to laugh as they did. A terrible necessity to be like the others goaded me into a desperate effort at that moment. I screwed my face to a grin. I must have looked grotesque as I stood there masking the unnatural grimace and bellowing guffaws.

After a second, I felt a pain in my throat and I became incapable of emitting any more of the forced laughter. My eyes were smarting and my dry lips were tasting salty tears. Both cheeks were wet and I felt a painful tightness in my chest. I had caught something of the agony in the contorting body and in the poor dull eyes of the dying beast. Yet, in that moment, when I fought a powerful longing to fall to the ground, embrace the suffering animal and weep over its quivering muzzle, I feared for myself. Had they discovered that I couldn't laugh? Did they know I was crying? I heard a bell ring. Recess was over and everyone scooted toward school. They hadn't noticed me. Ah! But I had!

Another day came when I stood in line to wait my turn at the toboggan slide. Jessie spied me and something seemed to cloud in my head as I saw her coming toward me. She tapped me on the shoulder as before, and ordered me to the rear of the line. The humiliating scene had been repeated many times—almost every time I ventured to avail myself of any pleasure. But this time I remembered the horse, and the crazy way I had denied myself—denied my true feelings to please others, to be like them. I felt strength surging through my body, and my mind was suddenly free of its fog. My voice came out clear and loud and I was not ashamed of it. "NO!" I said. Jessie's jaw sagged, making her lips a gaping oval. In a flash, composure was restored and the same lips stretched around gritting teeth. Those around us giggled.

Her further demands all met with my determined refusal. Then she threatened me, choosing words that were meant to shoot terror through my being. I stood. Her first angry fist banged my ear. I didn't know where I hit her. All I knew was that my fists were flying fast, and I suddenly discovered I was winning. Jessie screamed for her cohorts to pitch in on me. Then I felt the buffeting of many pairs of fists, and my shins pained from kicks, too.

How long I would have endured under this onslaught, I don't know. Emma, a large girl and older than anyone in the group, rushed in the midst, objecting, "It ain't fair! No bunch of kids should beat up on one! Let Jessie and the little one go to it." We did, and Jessie soon hollered, "I give up. Stop!" I was glad to stop. The crowd cheered and applauded, and as I wiped my handkerchief over my scratched cheeks, I could see admiring eyes. Walking home from school that afternoon, I felt I had fought for and found self-respect, but I was not deeply satisfied. There was something wrong about all this. Mother had said girls shouldn't fight. I was ashamed to talk about this at home.

Despite my newly acquired, hard-won status, I remained a child alone in a crowd of savagely excitable older children. I could not seem to catch their excitement and I completely lacked the enthusiasm they had for running, jumping, scampering around and giving vent to gibbering squeals. The boys, whose playground was adjacent, were much the same, I observed, only rougher and louder. I remained alone.

In our art class at school, we were drawing pictures of birds in soft pastel colors. I loved this and excelled. Always the teacher would rush to my desk after the allotted time assigned for drawing and hold my work high for all to see and admire. These squirming kids had their sober moments, and this was one of them. There would be *Oohhhs* and *Ahhhs* in tones that would pale the eloquence of art critics. They liked my drawings. Compliments were difficult for me. When a schoolmate said "That's sure a swell picture," I could feel my cheeks burn as I would venture some depreciating remark—"Oh, it isn't so good." But I thought it *was* good, and was very pleased that everyone else did.

Emma, the large girl who had rescued me from the pack the day of my fight with Jessie, sat directly in front of me. It was a poor seating arrangement to place the tallest girl in the room right in front of one smaller in stature, but that is how it was. I had to crane my neck and lean out toward the aisle if I wanted a view of the teacher from time to time. But in drawing, the large cardboard bird picture to be copied was always fastened to the blackboard, which was along the side of the room instead of up front. There was no straining for a view of the model and I worked very contentedly.

On one occasion, Emma turned around in her seat, as was her habit, to see how I was progressing. She always said some nice thing about my drawing, but even this made me nervous. I hated being watched while working, but I tried not to show annoyance. On this day, Emma remarked, "Time is almost up and you haven't got feet on the bird." Irritated, I quickly promised, "I know. I'm doing that next." With black chalk between her fingers, her arm came across my desk and to my horror, my lovely bird was marred by the marking of two straight lines like stilts under the creature's graceful little body. At the bottom of these lines she drew forks.

"There," she said with satisfaction, "that finishes it." My heart sank. The disappointment was keen, for then the teacher tapped her desk-bell and called, "Time is up!" As always, she came to my desk first. I watched her eyes and saw instantly the disappointment. She flung the drawing back. "You've ruined it! Why did you draw legs like that?" I did not answer, because I could not think of anything to say. Emma was my friend. Well, we weren't chums, but hadn't she championed me? I could not tell on Emma.

I just sat there. The teacher shrugged and passed down the aisle, admiring and correcting drawings as she went. Occasionally I could hear someone asking why my drawing had not been shown to the class. I couldn't hear her answer because the blood began to pound in my temples. I was angry. Strangely, I was not angry at Emma. I was not angry at the teacher, either. Emma had meant well, and the teacher was right in saying the drawing was ruined. But I had a very bitter feeling of defeat. Was I not to succeed in anything? Would something always spoil things for me?

⁓

Attending this large elementary school, my ears had heard unfamiliar words sometimes whispered, sometimes shouted. I knew there was something wrong about those words. I did not know exactly how to act when someone spoke them in my hearing. I fell to watching other faces and imitating their snickers and smirks. I wanted to know what I was pretending to know, and so I asked my mother. She saw it was time to teach me about sex before I would hear all about it in gutter terms. She frankly gave as complete an explanation as I could receive at my age, emphasizing the immorality of it outside of wedlock. I barely understood and I recoiled from the mental pictures this conversation brought to mind.

I wanted to forget I had ever heard it—that my own mother had told me. She had said that it was all right for married people.

When I became a little older, I was to have another such conversation with my mother, this time unsolicited by me. It could hardly be called a conversation, really. I just sat and listened while she explained about the evil diseases transmitted through illicit sex acts and the calamity of bringing a child into the world unfathered. These things I would not have been able to grasp at the age of my earlier inquiry. I felt uncomfortable about the explanation and ventured to ask only one question, and I couldn't find words to phrase that.

"You and Daddy—I mean—" I stammered.

It was then Mother told me how they had agreed to abstain from this relationship after my conception. While she was telling me this, I was also learning something else. I learned that I had not been wanted.

The cutting sadness was dulled by the focus of my mind on my mother's purity. She was not a partaker of this shameful act. Not now, anyway. To me, Mother was the embodiment of all that was right, pure and decent.

When at the end of the talk she said, "Now Jane, you have not been left in ignorance. There is no reason that you should ever fall," I felt as if I were perched on a precipice. It was time for me to speak. It was time for me to say, "Mother, I shall never fall." But the insecurity I felt urged no such speech. Maybe in an effort to arouse in me the determined assurance she expected, she added, "If you ever get into trouble, I could never have sympathy for you. You would be without excuse." I was glad this talk had ended.

My father too, felt a responsibility to enlighten me. Had not Mother told me first, I would never have guessed what all his talk about the birds and bees meant. He, too, had an appropriate denouement. "Jane, now you know. But if you are ever in trouble—any trouble—come to me! I've told you these things so that you need not be overtaken in ignorance, but if you are weak and if you fall, come to me!"

I was staring at him. I asked, "Even if I'm wrong, if I'm at fault, should I still come?"

Tears were in his eyes. "Dear Child," he said, "even if you are so wrong that you are hated by everyone and you even hate yourself—come to me. I will always love you and I will always help."

Chapter Three

Father was good to Mother in many ways. His sign business did not bring much money; nevertheless, he insisted all laundry be sent out. He believed that a woman with the responsibility of motherhood should not have the added burden of drudgery over a washtub (the way laundry was done in those days). He also believed that a married woman should not share in the breadwinning. My mother never had to find a job out in the workplace.

"It is the man's place to provide for his family," he said.

This was all very well, but Father had some other convictions that were not quite so favorable for Mother. He believed women should not be allowed to drive automobiles or vote. The hardest for Mother to accept was his insistence that women should not contribute to the support of the church.

"Men earn the money, and if there is any giving to be done, only the man has a right to give."

In our family, "the man" did not choose to go to church at all. If Mother wished to go, he did not forbid, but he would not consent to her contributing financially. He would allow Mother and me ten cents each. The coin did not indicate stinginess, for it had nothing to do with giving. It was a face-saving token for Mother and me when the offering plate was passed.

In some services, urgent pleas were made for funds. At such times I shared Mother's embarrassment when everyone in the congregation but Mother could stand and pledge. Sundays Mother took to reading the Bible to me at home. I was interested as she read and expounded. Father, too, read from the Bible. "Every educated person should be acquainted with Scripture," he would say. But he also read from Bob Ingersoll's compiled lectures on atheism. One parent taught me to believe while the other persuaded me to be an unbeliever. It got so that Mother and I read together, but Father and I studied together, turning pages of the Bible to confirm Ingersoll's alleged contradictions of Scripture.

I was about thirteen when Mother took me to hear Aimee Semple McPherson, the famous evangelist from Los Angeles, who spoke to record crowds filling the Coliseum in Chicago. We had to stand in line to hear her, waiting outside until the evangelist had spoken to a capacity audience; then another capacity audience was let in. Through life I hated crowds and mobs, and standing in lines, but when inside, spellbound under the impact of the speaker's dynamic delivery, I esteemed the standing and waiting but trivial.

I responded to her message in every way—even to her invitation to accept Christ.

"The way she puts it—she's so sincere. There must be a God. I want to be on her side. I'll accept Christ as she asks." I would have done anything the evangelist asked. Mother was in ecstasy.

Home with my dad, I was bold to declare all I had learned under the ministry of the evangelist. Father listened without interrupting. He did not seem disappointed, nor did his manner indicate that he favored my fervent declarations of faith. He just listened in silence.

Later—after I had gushed forth all that had spurred the enthusiasm, I felt dry and a little embarrassed. I noticed him watching me. Once, when I caught his eye, I saw him grinning. To my inquiring look he said, "I was just chuckling to myself. You are a Christian now, you say?"

I felt uncomfortable. "No—er—I didn't say that. I only said I know there is a God."

"But you accepted Christ."

I began to qualify—to apologize. "That doesn't mean I believe the Bible or that I'm going to join church or anything like that. I just think that Jesus was a good man. He must have been. And, oh, Dad—if you had heard how she explained everything…"

He picked me up at that point. "That is it, my dear! 'How she explained everything!' You were captivated by a powerful personality. You have not experienced conversion. You have experienced a phase of religious fervor. It will pass."

I was ashamed. I can now tell you sorrowfully, the religious fervor *did* pass.

Students at the high school I attended were strictly disciplined and well behaved. My nervous system suffered no shock from squirmings and screams as was the case in elementary school. Yet, I did not seem able to mix well with others. Conversation didn't come easily. Girls talked about dating, parties and dresses, and I didn't find any of these interesting. I had no dates. My parents didn't feel I was old enough to have boyfriends, and as sentinels, they scooted away any young male who even looked as though he might come calling.

My dresses were remade from those an aunt in Kansas City sent to Mother. Painstakingly, Mother toiled hours to achieve the modern look I insisted upon, or I would not have worn them. But I was not pleased with my clothes. I knew they were made-over, and I thought that everyone else did. For this reason I declined all party invitations. Mother was not disappointed in this, but Father was. He wanted me in the swing of things, he said.

"I'll not go if I have to wear these rags!" I would storm when he pressed me.

We sat two-at-a-desk in many of our classes in school, and I was constantly being seated with a girl by the name of Gertrude. Her last name had the same alphabetical beginning as my own—thus the seating arrangement. She was a nice tidy girl, but she had a chronic habit of giggling. No humorous event was needed to provoke it, either. She giggled at everything. It annoyed me to distraction, for when her giggling face bobbed before me, I felt that I should be giggling also. At last I tried. There wasn't any heart in my giggle, but I was being sociable.

After a week or so of this practice, I became quite good at it. I was able to giggle as though I were tickled. Then a strange thing happened. Gertrude's face sobered. There was practically no giggling from her, and soon there was none at all. She fell silent, and it was unmistakable in the cafeteria and in classes where we were not seated together that she was avoiding me. This bothered me, for I had no idea of the cause. What had I done? I confronted her with her change of manner. She hesitated, but I insisted on knowing.

"All right," she said, "I'll tell you. You're too silly. You giggle about nothing. It makes me nervous."

I wanted to take hold of her shoulders and shake her good. I wanted to shout, "You! You're the silly fool! You giggled so much I tried to learn to giggle so that I could stand you. I tried to giggle like *you*!"

But I didn't say any of this. I turned my back and walked away, and that day I turned away from ever trying to be like anyone else.

Free from seeking to melt myself into a pattern of conformity, I plunged into the happier business of being myself. I enjoyed my studies and gave myself to them. I became an honor student and counselor of my class. That was the highest-class office to be had, and I was proud. So was Dad. Mother's enthusiasm never matched ours, for she had other objectives in mind for me—spiritual ones.

In the later years of my adolescence, I had overcome some of my shyness. While I didn't have scores of friends, I had a few who were close. I did well in school and was especially interested in art and journalism. A community newspaper offered me part-time employment. I covered some civic meetings and even interviewed Uldine Utley, the child evangelist, whose personality I lauded in my column. But most of all, I enjoyed interviewing stage and screen celebrities and writing about their lives, their tastes and their talents.

My father turned over to me some of his reproduction art assignments and I found delight in doing this type of work. And I did it well. My father beamed. Mother was not given to eulogy, but her comments showed that she was pleased, too. I was really happy.

There were plenty of flaws in me—flaws that even I could see. I wasn't exactly quick-tempered, but I was certainly hot-tempered. When I felt that injustices (as I conceived them) had piled too high, I would give way to an outburst. Sharp, unkind words tumbled from my lips, and at times I would double my fist and pound on the table or desk or the wall. Father took this lightly. "Blowing off steam," he called it. But Mother called it an ungodly temper.

Father had a way of studding his conversation with gems of wit. When I read or heard a bit of current news, I always enjoyed discussing things with him so that I could listen to him talk. Whether on the light side or serious, his metaphors were vivid; he had a flair for words. I was fascinated by the way he could invest the mundane with a special glow—or so it seemed to my emerging mind. In sarcasm, one could taste the spice and sting of his high seasoning, and where some would be given ulcers, I found it palatable. Ulcers would surely have found lodgment in the stomachs of the clergy, for most of his sardonic wit was directed against religion and the church. While accepting his sparkling speech, I accepted also his doctrines.

Soon I stopped accompanying Mother to church. Father would not allow Mother to demand my attendance or to coax me. "She is free to go if she desires," he said, "but I will not allow her to be compelled."

Mother knew she was losing. At times I came upon her in our bedroom. Grieved and distressed, she knelt praying aloud for my father's and my salvation. This humble posture struck me as groveling. I had no respect for one who groveled, and groveling before a non-existent God repelled me. In my mind, I wove the thorny crown of denunciation for her bowed head. A wave of disgust rushed over me to be succeeded by a wave of pity. I actually felt merciful when I sought to arouse her from the act of supplication.

"Mother, Mother! Stop now and look up at me. No one hears you praying. No one except me. There's no one else in this room. There is no God, Mother. Can't you see there's nothing to it? That dark superstitious book—that Bible you read—is responsible for all this."

The kneeling figure remained and the tears continued to flow, though her prayerful words ceased to be audible. She did not stop praying, but she knew Father had won a disciple to atheism.

Chapter Four

Mother had been ill for two weeks from blood poisoning. A simple cut on her thumb from a can opener had caused the infection. Her hand and arm had swollen stiff, and when salves and hot applications failed, the doctor ordered her to the County Hospital.

Visiting hours were restricted, so I saw her only once. She did not talk much, and when I asked how she felt, she smiled faintly. At home, I told my father all this, adding, "But her eyes were glassy, Dad. Why do you suppose that is?"

He frowned thoughtfully and said, "It could be the sedatives they are giving to relieve pain."

But that night he sat in his chair, silently staring until we went to bed. A few mornings later, I answered the telephone. The voice on the other end of the wire asked for Mr. William Page or Jane Page. "I am Jane Page," I said.

Then I was told to come at once to the hospital—"Your mother is dying." That was all.

I do not remember what I said after that, or if I just hung up the receiver and wept. My father took over the job of thinking.

It was the year the banks failed all over the country—the beginning of the Great Depression. We could not afford a taxi, even at a time like this. Before we boarded a street-car, Father wired Raymond, my half-brother. At the large, busy, overcrowded hospital, we were directed to one of the side rooms stemming from a corridor. There, behind a screen on a white narrow bed, my mother lay dying.

Aunt Laura, my mother's sister from Kansas, was there at the bedside. I was surprised that she knew. My dad, I learned, had wired her the night I told him Mother's eyes were glassy. It would be a matter of minutes, the nurse said frankly. I did not greet my aunt, but bent over Mother's perspiring forehead. I wanted very much at that moment to pray. I thought of asking God—the God whose existence I had denied, but who now seemed very real—to save my mother from dying. Instead, I turned to the nurse, imploring, "Save her! Please don't let her die!" Then I turned to the doctor who had approached and I pleaded with him. He brushed past me to the bedside. I heard Aunt Laura say, "Nettie is in heaven."

Father stood silent. I began to sob and my aunt cried, too. We did not linger in the room, but took the elevator downstairs. I was too shaken to enter into conversation. I heard my aunt tell Father that she and Uncle Herbert would come over to our apartment later that day. Father and I walked to where we would get our streetcar back home. Neither of us spoke; there seemed to be nothing to say.

In the moving traffic, the smiles and nods and busy chatter of people who talked and greeted one another along the street disturbed me. Why was everything going on just as though nothing had happened? My mother was gone! My world had stopped. Why was their world still going on? I realized then that I loved my dear mother. Oh, how I would miss her!

In silence, Father and I sat side by side in the streetcar. We would return together to our lonely apartment, and we both dreaded this.

I looked blankly out the window, seeing a blur of houses and stores, as the streetcar rolled along narrow tracks. I wasn't seeking sight of anything, particularly, but my eyes fell on a sign. A sign hung in a little mission window, upon which was printed, "MOTHER'S PRAYERS WILL FOLLOW." Somehow, that sent electrical vibrations down my spine. I did not know why, but that sign was speaking to me, telling me something. Did that mean that the prayers I had mocked, my mother's prayers over which I had ranted, were going to mean something in my life? I asked myself, "Why should that sign come to view at this particular moment?"

When I reached home, I turned to the flyleaf of my Bible—the same Bible Father and I had studied in atheistic light. I hand-printed the words I had seen in the mission window, "MOTHER'S PRAYERS WILL FOLLOW."

I was crying when I put the Book down. Then less exalted thoughts came to me, which I accepted. This was a time of stress. I had indulged in a mood and gesture of sentiment which was excusable at a time of grief. I would not censure myself, but I would not be overcome. I must close the Bible, and in so doing, close my heart and mind to yearnings about eternity and visions of meeting Mother again in some great beyond. I told myself I had learned to my own satisfaction that such concepts were unsound—tenants only of an emotional state of mind. I would take myself in hand and entertain no more such transient thoughts.

My own dear mother, whom I mourned, was herself a classic example of the futility of the Christian life, I thought. What pleasure or fun had she? She and my father had lived as strangers—not as happily mated married people. I regretfully remembered how unkindly I had railed upon her for her pains in sewing dresses for me out of Aunt Laura's clothing. Many of her tasks of mending, sewing, cooking and neat housekeeping were just taken for granted by Dad and me. We hardly ever commented and I knew we seldom thanked her.

Especially in recent years, her unhappiness had become apparent. I had come upon her many times kneeling at the bedside in tears. There had been no joy, no happiness, none of the thrills of life for her that I could see. I concluded that the dear woman's life, though noble and unselfishly lived, was pitifully wasted. I determined that however reverent my memories of her, I would not emulate that life. I wanted to live for pleasure, happiness, fun, and good times.

I expressed to Dad my desire to get out of Chicago for a while. I feared the loneliness and depression that would settle upon me if I remained in familiar surroundings where Mother had so recently shared life with my father and me.

Aunt Laura offered to take me to live with her and Uncle Herbert in their home in Kansas City. Father objected. He insisted that if I went anywhere, it would be Toledo, Ohio, to live with his sister and her family. He had talked to his sister by telephone and tentative plans had been made. I really wanted to go with Aunt Laura, because I had known her and Uncle Herbert in earlier childhood. I had always liked Aunt Laura and held Uncle Herbert in awe and respect. Aunt Laura won my affection when, on one occasion, she had looked at me with her keen brown eyes and said, "I like you, Jane, not as a relative, but as a friend. There is a difference. Your friends you can choose, but your relatives, you can't."

That was said years ago when I was quite young, but it made me feel I had a friend in my Aunt Laura. Father's folks I had never met. But Father insisted that he would consent to my leaving only to go to his sister. So Aunt Laura and Uncle Herbert returned to Kansas City without me.

The few days I was with my father's folks in Toledo were a nightmare. Father's elderly sister avoided me entirely. Her sons and daughters soon told me their mother had been impulsive when she invited my father to send me there. The management of the home and finances had been out of her hands for years, they explained. They accused Father of being presumptuous in accepting his sister's polite offer. His sister, Molly, had said afterwards that she had made the offer thinking it a polite and proper thing to do at a time of death, but she never dreamed Billy would have the nerve to accept. I learned for the first time that it was Molly's husband's money that supported my father's deserted wife and children years before.

"What is he doing now—sending another of his off-spring for us to keep?"

All this was told to me two days after my arrival. I was numb. To soothe me, they said they knew this was not my fault. Then one of them asked, "Jane, how long do you plan to stay?"

Without hesitation I answered, "Just as long as it takes me to pack up my few things and get out of here."

They didn't expect that. They didn't like it, either. They became a little worried and tried to persuade me to stay until my father could be reached by phone or wire. They even tried to tone the whole thing down, and pretended they wanted me for a visit.

As I left, they became quite angry. "What will your father say?"

"What do you care?" I snapped. "You don't like him anyway."

I would not accept the money one of them offered. I had enough for bus fare to Rockwood, Michigan, where my brother Raymond and his wife lived. It was not far from Toledo.

Raymond and his wife, Lillian, welcomed me warmly. Under their shepherding care, thoughts of faith in God and in a hereafter dawned again in my mind. The devotions and worship services I attended with them were not annoying, for they gave me a feeling of being loved. At times, I thought that I, too, believed in God. Then at other times, I felt that I didn't believe. At any rate, to have eternal life in heaven and to meet Mother again was lovely to contemplate, so I accepted it—if not in fact, at least as a possibility. Thus I passed from atheism to agnosticism.

There was restlessness in me. I was not content to sit in Raymond and Lillian's home and do nothing. I felt the need to chart my own course in life—to busy myself doing something. I told them I wanted to go back to Chicago. While my welcome in their home was assured, Lillian and Raymond consented that my decision to be self-sustaining was normal and right. I said goodbye, mindful of their open hearts and home, and free from a burden of obligation to remain or to repay them in any way for their willing hospitality.

Back in Chicago, I told my Dad how his folks had treated me. He was sorry his plans fell through, concerning my stay with his sister, and was quite enraged at the family's conduct toward me. As far as I know, he never communicated with any of those people again.

I can't explain why, but I had lost interest in art and writing at this point and sought other types of work. I took a job in a printing establishment, but quit when the proprietor stepped up the speed of the press. It was a hand-feeder, but automatic in the sense that it could be set to various speeds. When a clean white sheet of paper was hand-placed in position for the heavy press to clamp its imprint, my hand had better be withdrawn—or else! At a slower speed I could manage, but when the speed was increased, I feared for the safety of my right hand.

While sharing a small apartment with my dad, I took jobs soliciting orders door-to-door, selling volumes of classics. I tried other sales jobs, too. I made average commissions, I guess, but I didn't like the work and I did not stick.

Chapter Five

When splashing in the mud, everything one pulls out—whether sticks or stones, either crude or polished—is mud-covered. So are the events of my life from this time up to my commitment in the Kankakee State Hospital. I have no desire to use my pen as a ladle to stir this muck and drag up everything in it. It is enough that I offer a fleeting outline of my adolescent years.

First there was Harold. Harold's steady blue eyes smiled as he talked. They smiled as he sat patiently and listened, too. There was an earnest manner about him that I liked. He said to me one day, "Jane, I'm not a church member, nor do I consider myself a good Christian. But I do believe we have a great and wonderful God and I feel that all the world should know of His goodness and love." I was listening, but no approving smile awarded his revealing declaration.

"Jane, I want to be a missionary, " he said rather desperately. "I don't know how to train—or how to go about this, or to what wild and uncivilized place I may go, but it seems right to me that I should serve God in this way."

Hitherto I had always admired the quiet strength and courage of Harold's personality, but after he told me that, I imagined I could see in him a weak and insipid mixture of Pollyanna and Don Quixote.

When later he proposed marriage, I was ready with my answer and the reason for my answer. "I wouldn't think of marrying any man foolish enough to want to waste his life suffering hardship and privation in some remote territory of the world to change the religion of savages."

After my break with Harold, I went steady with Mark for a while. His worldly-wise wit and charm was indeed a contrast to Harold's calm spirit, but I found Mark much to my liking. His impetuous love for parties and good times intrigued me. He was always ready for a lark of some kind. He enjoyed gambling and he drank, too. I shared his pleasure in all these activities.

In spite of Mark's spirited personality, he seemed to have moods given to intensive concentration and was capable of deep sincerity. He was marvelously gifted on the violin—a protegé of Fritz Chrysler.

We became engaged to be married, but I broke the engagement one day when he accused me of going out with other men. I had accepted dates with older men, men of thirty-five and forty years old, although I was still in my teens. My father did not know this. I would sneak out at night, or I would lie, saying I was with a girlfriend. I found the flattery of these men very pleasant and their glossy courtesies delightful. Mark was by no means vulgar or crude, but at twenty, his speech lacked the urbanities of these sophisticated escorts. Nor did he open doors, place chairs, etc., with their practiced deference.

When Mark angrily accused me, I shouted, "Yes, Mark! And I intend to go out with men any time I like. You're just a punk kid—not a mature man! We're both too young to tie ourselves in marriage."

After this stormy rebuff, Mark fell to docile pleadings— then most tender entreaties. At last, Mark saw that I had meant every word. As he left he said, "May God help you! I thank God that I found this out before our marriage."

I met and became fascinated with all types of fast-living characters. Some sparkled like rhinestones, and though I knew they were not jewels, I liked their glitter nevertheless. Others were of a cruder cut—even vulgar— but they charmed me, too.

Finally, on my downward spiral, I left my dad to live with "Stripper Sal." She had been much publicized for her manner of robbery. At the point of a gun, she drove her victims way out to the country and ordered them to strip. Then, taking their clothes and valuables, she would drive off in her car, leaving them naked and stranded. That was her way of ensuring a clean "get-away" with the loot.

When I moved in with her, she had retired from these dramatic activities and had settled down in a neat quiet little racket, but she displayed her news clippings with the same pride a champion treasures trophies.

After Harold and Mark, there were other boyfriends. Not boys, usually, but worldly men "on the make." I soon learned to suspect ulterior motives behind every gift, invitation, attention, and courtesy. I became cynical, and when I found a man whose fondness for me was real, I would make the most of his ardor to serve my purpose—to meet whatever need I had at the moment.

I met more and more racket people, and soon got into rackets myself. Sometimes I had the illusion of being on top—"in the bucks." I had cars, I traveled, I had everything—or so I told myself.

Driving around the country became one of my passions. I would decide for no reason at all that I would like to go to San Francisco, or to Phoenix, to Detroit, or New York—and I would get into my car and drive there. Usually some irresponsible idler or two would accompany me on such trips, for I never liked to be alone.

On occasion, when I happened to be driving in the vicinity of Detroit near Rockwood, Michigan, where my half-brother and his wife lived, I would stop and see them for about twenty minutes or so. I was never quite sure whether these very brief visits were prompted by my gratitude for their kindness to me after Mother's death, or simply that I wanted to show off my lovely clothes and new car.

Since my friends were along, I knew they would have to be introduced, and so I'd venture an apology for my brother's religion. In an effort to have my friends accept my brother and his wife, I would painfully explain that Raymond and Lillian were really nice people—"hearts of gold, but there is one thing wrong with them." I felt uncomfortable mentioning it; it seemed a confession that might reap ridicule from my friends. Apologetically I would explain, "They are both a little off on religion." Someone in the group was usually quick to offer comfort: "Don't feel too badly about that, Jane. After all, it isn't your fault, and there's usually one or two like that in almost every family."

Thus I was consoled, and my shame concerning Raymond and Lillian's religion abated. But there were times I felt that I should deal with this weakness in my brother and sister-in-law. "You're really too involved in this religion of yours," I would criticize. "You're just fanatics, that's all! Just crazy religious fanatics!"

This hurt them, I knew. I could see it in their eyes. But after leaving, I would wonder. Were they hurt because my words had revealed to them the fanaticism to which they had fallen—or were they hurt because I couldn't see and couldn't share the exalted experience they had?

They never turned me away; they never retaliated unkindly; they never questioned the caliber of my friends, nor the truthfulness of my boasts, and yet all the while I had a feeling that these two people could see clear through me.

It wasn't long before the "breaks" stopped coming my way. I lamented that my luck had changed. Things got steadily worse, and as they did, I took to drinking more and more. At first I was certain I could stop, or at least cut down any time I wanted to; but soon I felt myself slipping into an abyss. I tried desperately to stop, but there was nothing to hold on to.

My shallow "good time" friends scurried. They saw me sinking and didn't want to be around when I called for help.

One night, I frantically knocked on my father's door and begged for my Bible. I had been drinking, but I was not as drunk as I was heartsick. My father refused. "Jane, I've kept it for sentiment, but I don't want to give it to you now. You will lose it in some bar room—or in your condition, you might even trade it for a drink."

But I persisted. At last he let me have the Bible, after he made me promise to return it to him.

I had been told that the Bible says that everyone is born with a fundamental goodness. My mother had never taught this, but I had heard others say it. At this time of acute suffering and distress, I felt I needed to know if I were any good at all. There was certainly no goodness within myself that I could see, but if a search through the Bible revealed that everybody was good, that would include me, too. And so I searched hungrily.

I could not find these reassuring passages about fundamental human goodness, but I did find many parts that said all have sinned and are lost.

I discussed all this with my close friend, Clara De Runtz, whose life was as sordid as my own, and whose poor mind was as drenched in alcohol as mine. "People lose their minds reading that Book," she warned me.

I had first met Clara back in 1931—the first time I had ever been arrested. Out on bail, I faced trial the next morning and I dropped in on a friend who would be a sympathetic listener. He introduced me to his visitor and I told them both about my troubles and arrest. Clara thought my worldly experience glamorous, just as I had once thought Stripper Sal's. I offered, as a reward for her admiration, a special treat: I invited her to go with me to court the next day.

The judge and then a social worker both scolded me. I was made to promise not to drink and was forbidden to associate with ex-convicts. I agreed to all this, tongue-in-cheek, and was freed. I was only sixteen.

Clara was five years older than I, but younger looking, and she was in most things naïve.

She was small in frame, of normal height, and very thin, but her lean little face was not unattractive under the curly cap of brown hair she wore in a short bob. Her eyes, though soft, were keenly alert. She thought I was clever— even brilliant—and this pleased me not a little.

I had other friends; we both had friends—friends who were no friends, really. Somehow, in spite of the mess Clara and I made of our lives, our friendship stuck.

We tried one racket after another, thinking ourselves smart. We really worked harder to avoid work than had we taken an honest job. And what a toll this hectic existence took of our nerves and distraught minds, accompanied by the torment we went through because of our drinking. We traveled all over the country together until we wound up back in Chicago, the city of our birth.

When I sought my doctor and asked for his help in overcoming my alcoholism, I learned that Clara had complained to him of my reading the Bible. He gravely advised me to stop reading. "Your life doesn't measure up to the standards of the book," the doctor explained, "and since you are incapable of changing, this Bible reading is only contributing to your distress of mind."

I begged him then to help me in whatever way he could. He offered to commit me to the psychopathic ward in Chicago, where I would be locked away and couldn't get alcohol for a while. Strange, but I consented to this. After being admitted, I was told by a psychiatrist examining me, "You are a hopeless alcoholic. You will never be any different."

I could not believe I was hearing right. Of course, I knew I was an alcoholic and I was tormented by strong, persistent doubts and fears that I would never be able to stop drinking. But how dare this man of medicine—a man supposedly dedicated to healing—how *dare* he torture me? Trembling as I was, devoid of strength, his remark had nevertheless kindled a flame of anger.

"Is this the way you help people?" I flared. "Is this how you ease suffering and offer encouragement? Is this what you tell every patient?"

He was unruffled. "No, I do not tell everyone they are hopeless, because everyone is not. But you are, and I am telling you the truth."

In that moment I hated this man, his science, and even the society that set him over me as judge of my mental state. He laughed when I told him I would quit drinking and get an honest job. "Who would hire you and for what?" he questioned.

Waves of wrath beat the blood to my temples, but sitting there in his presence, shaking, trembling—almost convulsing—I knew my talk about reform made the spectacle that I was, a comedy.

At the conclusion of this interview, I knew that I was destined to be sent away and locked up where I would not be able to get alcohol for quite some time.

Chapter Six

The unhappy reverie of my past was interrupted as one of the patients tapped me on the shoulder. "Time for a game?" I looked up into the hard lines of her pockmarked face. There was a curl to her lips that passed for a smile.

I played up to the irony of her question. "Time? I've time on my hands and I don't mean a wristwatch!"

As the cards were dealt, I was thinking of that transfer to 8-North and what had caused it.

I grumbled. "No fun playing without bets—but look at the trouble...." I moaned aloud: "O God! I must make my father see that he can't let them transfer me to that miserable ward."

"Come on! Come on!"

I saw the irritated frown of my card partner.

"It's your bid."

A torrent of words tumbled from my lips when my father visited. "Dad, they're going to transfer me to a horrible ward. There are dangerous patients there. Please! Oh, I beg you—please go to the head office and tell them not to do this!"

There was absence of joy in my father's patient smile. "Jane, they know what is best for you, dear. Nothing will harm you. We must not interfere."

All my pleadings would not budge him. My anger only bewildered him, and my tears made him cry, too. But he would not do as I asked. Hating him and hating myself because I couldn't manage to hate him as much as I wanted to, I wept bitterly. I was weeping when he left and continued sobbing long hours after he had gone.

An attendant sought to comfort. "Jane, don't feel so bad. I'm going to take you over to the other ward myself and when I do, I'll introduce you to someone. When you meet this person, everything will be all right. You will see."

Grasping hungrily for any crumb of comfort, I felt lifted. But curiosity prodded me to ask, "Who is this person?"

I wondered if the person were a doctor or a social worker. Or maybe she had in mind some kindly attendant. But not even in the throes of delirium tremens would I have imagined her to name the person she did.

"Maude Oberg!"

Maybe it was the way I looked that caused her to ask hastily, "Have you heard of Maude?"

I shuddered. I certainly had! Maude Oberg was notorious for her life of crime. She was known as "Angel Face" to the nightlife of Chicago. When she was a young woman of twenty-two, she had stabbed and killed a man. Now fifty years old, Maude was in the State Hospital for drug addiction.

I recalled my first sight of Maude Oberg at Kankakee.

Muriel, hospitalized for attempted suicide, had urged me to go to one of the patient dances. There was a large hall on the grounds that was used for church services and recreation. Dances were scheduled on Friday nights. Patients who chose to go lined up under the escort of a recreational therapist who later returned them to their home wards.

Muriel had said, "Really, you should get off the home ward and have what fun there is to be had around here. You'll meet lots of interesting people at the dance." She described how the men sat in rows of seats on one side of the dance floor and the women on the other. At a signal, the men rushed to pick partners among the women.

"After you've gone a few times, "Muriel had smiled, "you will get to know some of the men, and you may get yourself a steady boyfriend like I have."

This prospect had not intrigued me but curiosity prompted me to consent to go. I chided Muriel for suggesting that interesting people would be there. "I said interesting, dearie, not noble," she giggled.

To impress me further, she led with a question: "Do you know who plays the piano at these dances?" I didn't know and didn't care, but Muriel was anxious to tell.

"None other than Maude Oberg—Angel Face of crime!"

Muriel was disappointed that recognition and interest didn't brighten my features. She knew that her next remark would not catch fire, but she offered it anyway.

"Maude is really a clever person; you should hear them clap when she walks across the floor to the piano."

So I allowed myself to be herded into the auditorium and seated among the women patients. Sights of ribbons on stringy, unkempt hair and drab, ill-fitting garments girded with bands of velvet and lace made me stare. Gaudy sashes circling flabby bellies could have been funny were not the sight so pathetic.

A loud burst of applause and much cheering and whistling directed my attention to the strutting figure of a woman crossing the dance floor. Smiling and waving, Maude Oberg had jewelry strung around her neck, pinned on her bosom, and circling her wrists. It flashed a gaudy sparkle as she made her way toward the platform. Auburn tints of hair made a shining frame for her big, bright smile. I was sitting quite a distance away and her features were hardly discernible, but the effect was all glitter and all smile.

She walked the full length of the auditorium. She could have mounted the platform and reached her piano from either side, but then the entrance would not have been as spectacular and the applause and screaming would not have lasted so long. It was evident that Maude wanted the full effect and enjoyed making it last.

When she sat down, the piano keys sounded a crescendo. They responded loudly to the pressure of her strong, nimble fingers. She pounded the keys with a fury, banging out rhythm. Her bobbing head kept smiling at the audience as her fingers tumbled and thumped.

But now they had stopped watching Maude. The men were rushing from their seats just as Muriel had said they would. They were a shabby lot, but at least no sprays of lace or faded ribbons made caricatures of them.

When at last I accepted an invitation to dance, I learned that my partner was subject to "spells." I could envision him having a seizure out there on the dance floor with me, haplessly entwined in arms and legs sprawling on the floor. I wanted to say "No thank you" the next time he asked, but I did not want to hurt his feelings. No frightening or embarrassing incident resulted, but I did feel like a kernel of popcorn hopping around in a skillet.

The patients' dancing techniques varied. They seemed to have acquired a knack of pairing up according to motor ability. Some just stood on the floor holding on to each other, swaying. They did not stand too close; that was against the rules, and attendants were watching. Others shuffled a very little, oblivious to the music. Couples leaped about in great sweeping movements, weaving in and out, dexterously avoiding knocking people down. There were also a few who danced well.

I could not help but notice that the doctors who sat in a special section of the auditorium were not searching for a breach in discipline as were the attendants; they were being entertained. There was no laughing, but the amusement on the doctors' faces was unmistakable.

I shook myself from this memory flashback. The attendant had asked if I had heard of Maude Oberg and was waiting to be answered. I must answer, I decided, in a way which would end this conversation, for I did not want my anger and confusion to show.

"Yes," was my simple reply.

She patted my shoulder, uttering a few more words she thought reassuring, and was gone.

Was this some cruel joke? How could an introduction to a woman such as Maude Oberg make everything all right for me? But then I was sure the attendant had not been joking. This was indeed an odd place where I should not have expected life to proceed normally, but certainly the attendants at least should evidence balanced thinking. Everything was so bewildering in this crazy, mixed-up world!

Why was a woman with a thinking apparatus like that paid by the state to be my keeper? I gritted my teeth at what I thought to be the injustice of it all.

Chapter Seven

My resentment found another target as I thought of my father's refusal to oppose my transfer. He could have pleaded for me, but would not. And now because he hadn't done as I asked, I would be locked up with raving maniacs and low characters—the elite of which was a woman of Maude Oberg's caliber! It was all so awful. I cried again. I could almost bring myself to wish something terrible would happen to me just to make my father sorry and ashamed. I knew that my suffering would make him suffer, and I was almost willing to pay the price. Almost.

The day soon came when the attendant who promised the introduction to Maude Oberg escorted me across the grounds to this dreaded ward. As I walked beside her I did not talk, for there was a lump in my throat.

As we entered the building, my offended eardrums vibrated with sudden noise. Loud voices and raucous laughter mingled with the din of chairs scraping the floor and feet stamping. Some patients just stood muttering incoherently and gesturing wildly, while others were prancing—there were even those who trotted about like ponies.

I stood there for a minute with my eyes closed. I heard the attendant who had delivered me talking with the ward attendant, but I paid slight attention to what they said. Then I heard the attendant call Maude's name. She was not heard above the racket. The ward attendant then clapped her hands and the more rational patients lowered their voices somewhat. Again she called, "Maude! Maude Oberg, come here."

I followed the attendant's gaze to the center of the room, and there beheld a group I had observed as the noisiest of all. The individual that towered head and shoulders above the others—and who, incidentally, had been making most of the noise—came toward us.

She had a booming voice and a beaming smile. I thought the smile was faked. I was presented to Maude and she was asked to show me the ropes. The attendant said, "This little girl isn't used to such a place. You take her under your wing, Maude."

Maude flashed her smile my way. I was not in a pliable mood, but I suddenly thought, "I was wrong about her smile. It is real."

The "wing" the attendant had solicited for my protection went into action immediately, for Maude slapped her arm around my shoulders. I shied at the rude jolt but managed to look pleasant.

Maude's loud voice sounded. "Cheer up, kid. You'll like it here. It will be like home to you after a while."

No! Not that! That I should ever be contented in such an atmosphere was a tormenting thought. How awful all this was. Again I was about to break out in great heaving sobs, and had to swallow hard to keep back the tears.

The next day, I was lined up with other patients and taken to another building where electric bulbs spotlighted rows of ironing boards. Apparently I had been assigned to work in the laundry. My place was pointed out and I was handed a bundle of blue shirts. The woman in charge said, "Iron these. These are patients' shirts. We will see how you do before we trust you with the doctors' laundry."

I had no yearnings for the promotion and no experience at all in wielding an iron. My iron skidded over wrinkles and buttons, and one of the patients observing nearby said, "Here, let me show you."

She neatly finished my pile. Before I could thank her, she flew back to her own board and when the laundry room supervisor appeared, I knew why. The woman looked at the beautiful outlay of work and exclaimed, "Oh, that's wonderful. Here!" As she sounded the last word, a hand was thrust toward me with new-looking white shirts. I took them, knowing something was wrong about all this, but what was I to do? Before I could think of anything to say, the supervisor was gone again.

The patient who had come to my aid before was busily engaged at her own ironing board. I tried to catch her eyes, which she kept carefully averted. I lacked the bravery to desert my post—or my board—to go over to her. There seemed to be only one other thing to do, and I did it—I ironed those two shirts. When I saw spots turning yellow, then deepening to brown, it was time to call the supervisor and explain. I did not have to call.

She appeared just at the right—or wrong—moment. The shrieking I had heard on my debut on Ward 8-North was nothing to be compared with the cry of horror from the supervisor as she held the two shirts at arm's length. It was then that I learned they were doctors' shirts. She had trusted them to me in view of the expert work she had supposed I had just done.

Visions of chains and bread and water came before me, but the supervisor, instead of thundering a rebuke, said to an attendant standing by, "It's my fault. I thought this one was just an alcoholic. But the poor thing is sick."

That night, the weather turned cold. It was February, and I was chilled on the narrow cot. I tried to wrap myself in the one blanket, but if I succeeded in warming my back, my feet were cold. When my feet were warm, my shoulders shivered. I asked the attendant for an extra blanket. I knew they had blankets, for I had noticed them the day before in a storage closet. She curtly refused. I hastened to tell her of the supply I had seen.

"Listen, you!" she snapped. "You ain't in any grand hotel. There's not enough blankets for all the patients to have two. Why should you get two? It's everybody or nobody!"

My fervent explanation about being cold-blooded and always suffering cold even when others were warm left her unimpressed.

She made no reply to my question—"As long as there are blankets, why not give them to patients who ask?"—and scowled over her shoulder as she walked away.

In the morning I had to visit the toilet—a place I hated because of its filth and lack of privacy. I stood in line trying not to look and not to inhale very deeply. It was a foul place. There were no partitions separating the toilet seats, trash littered the floor, and the odor of stale air plus the sight of unwashed receptacles and scum around the basins made me nauseous. There were creeping things on the walls and on the floors. I could recognize the roaches, but I did not know the names of the other species.

When my turn came, I discovered there was no toilet paper. Hating to lose my turn, I asked one of the patients, "Will you ask the attendant for paper?" She stared blankly. I had asked the wrong one. I asked another. She said, "Did you ever hear my husband sing, 'Oh Johnny'?" Then I raised my voice, addressing all—anyone who would hear and could understand—"Will someone please get toilet paper?"

I got my answer. "They ain't got any."

No one left the room, and not thinking it possible to ignore this need, I forfeited my turn and searched the dormitory for the attendant. She gave me a stony look. "There's no paper on the ward right now," she answered in a hard, metallic voice.

"But then you must get some here right away," I pleaded.

"The night woman should have ordered it, but she didn't. I haven't time right now. Go away and don't bother me."

"But—but—all those patients without toilet paper!" I stammered. Then, heatedly, I demanded, "You've got to get paper over here. You must!" She swung her big bulk menacingly toward me. "You just shut up!" she barked. "Who do you think you are, giving orders around here?"

Suffering the discomfort of a painful bladder, I was herded with the other patients over to the laundry. Immediately, I asked the supervisor for toilet paper. She obligingly untwined about seven or eight yards. "I'll not need that much," I protested. "Take it," she offered generously. "You'll need it through the day and back on your ward tonight."

What was she saying? I soon learned that toilet paper was a scarcity on the home wards, and the patients who went to working wards during the day got the benefit of yards of it to stuff into their pockets. In the working wards, rolls of toilet paper were unwound and doled out each day, and at the end of every week, male and female patients alike also received wads of chewing tobacco.

Patients joked about the toilet paper and tobacco being pay for their work, but it was a joke with a catch—the catch being that it was actually so.

I took my tobacco to Maude. "You can have it," I said, "I don't chew." Maude was genuinely concerned. "Well, you should learn, kid. Smokes are few and a chew of tobacco now and then satisfies that craving, you know." She was extending her hand for me to take it back. "No," I waved in refusal, "I can't use it."

"Maybe you have plenty of money to buy cigarettes and don't need this?" she smilingly asked. That was not so, and I hastened to inform Maude of my depleted "trust fund." Then I saw that Maude was doing me a kindness. She offered to teach me how to chew and also to dip snuff. Snuff was not nearly as expensive as cigarettes. My money was getting low—there being no source of replenishment, I decided to let Maude teach me. Gratitude—so strange a tenant in my heart—actually became alive as I considered how kind she was to tutor me in this art.

But when Maude's cheek pouched to a bulge, I despaired. It was not a picturesque act, nor did I have much of a stomach for it. I made a few futile, choking efforts, then Maude dismissed her failing protegé. But it seemed a shame not to be able to use my "salary."

Maude was a tall woman. She was always gaudily rouged, and even in that place she managed to sparkle with costume jewelry lavishly adorning her neck, wrists, and fingers. Her hair was bobbed to her earlobes and was rather straight, with a swirl to it here and there. It was darkish, but auburn tints flashed in the sunlight. The color was not artificial. Maude was underweight, but a suggestion lingered of former beauty.

The hardness of her features spoke of a life of kicks and beatings rather than cruel cunning. With the hard lines, there were creases of worry and thought and—if one looked really searchingly—great and deep sadness, too. Her voice was low and vibrant and commanded attention. When she sang even barrelhouse ditties and ballads for the patients, there was music in her tones and pathos, too. You felt something when you listened.

Saturday nights on the ward were set aside as "party time" for the patients, when for about an hour Maude entertained. She played and sang. Patients sang, too, and they danced, and even the attendants enjoyed Maude's music. It seemed that during Maude's "party time," the very disturbed patients would quiet down—some would sway to the rhythm or just stand in the middle of the floor and smile.

I liked Maude. But in spite of the cheer and encouragement of her presence, I despaired. Maude could not actually feel at peace in this place, I knew. She was speaking with a pretended optimism when she had said I would like it here. But Maude had better ability to adjust than I did. I just could not endure it, and I could not pretend. I did not even want to try.

I had two visitors. My aged father came at times. Apparently he had so adjusted his thinking that he found comfort in the thought that I was locked up and protected. He was told I would have destroyed myself if allowed the liberty to continue drinking. He had hoped for better things for me, a better way of life, but since I had persisted in wild living and drunkenness, he concluded this institution must be regarded as a blessing. His role from now on was to visit me and say what he could to encourage my contentment. This he managed to do with no show of exuberance.

Very gently and lovingly, he would say, "Jane dear, in here you do not have to face problems at all. Everything is all planned for you and provided for you. If you would only look at it that way, dear, you would see that you have it easy."

But I never looked at it that way, and when my father said things like this, I wondered if he considered me "gone" mentally. But I knew he loved me and I had disgraced him and robbed him of hope for any success in the life of his daughter. I pitied him because of his disappointment in me, and I burned with shame.

Clara, my other visitor, knew I was aware of her inability to help, but I urged her to influence and to even beg others to come to my aid. I always got a strong whiff of alcohol as Clara whispered close to my face, "Jane, now just be patient. I know a bartender who knows a politician, and we will pull a few strings and you'll be out of here in no time!"

As she talked, Clara was staggering. I urged her to sit down quickly before an attendant noticed.

Disgusted, I said, "Yes, Clara, you said that right. You'll have me out of here in no time! NO TIME is what I fear! You can't help yourself—how can you help me? Look at those two black eyes. It is a wonder they let you in. Seriously, how *did* you get past the desk to see me?"

Clara had expected gratitude for her pains in traveling the eighty-five miles from Chicago to Kankakee, and she was in no mood for this. She frowned angrily. "Do you want me to leave right now? I will, you know."

I was about to argue further when I noticed two of the attendants talking to a ward doctor. "Wait here," I said, and left Clara sitting alone while I maneuvered into a position to eavesdrop. I heard bits of their conversation. They were indeed discussing Clara's black eyes and her drunkenness, and I feared they were considering examining her for commitment.

I hastened to Clara. "Get going," I urged. "They are talking about keeping you here." Clara turned white and walked out without staggering. "What a sobering thought," I chuckled to myself.

When Clara came again, she had the smell of whiskey on her breath but she was not staggering drunk. One of her black eyes had cleared up quite well, and the other was heavily camouflaged with grease paint. I was proud of my visitor this time.

"Clara," I said, "I'm going to introduce you to Maude Oberg." She raised her hand in protest, but before she could say anything I had sought out Maude and brought her to the porch. I could not have made a more elaborate introduction were the scene taking place in the White House. But my friends were not responding.

Clara stretched out a limp hand that Maude, after hesitating, shook reluctantly. Neither spoke. They just stared at each other. Finally, Maude said, "Well, I have to go now." Clara did not detain her. "Goodbye", she said. Maude looked displeased and nodded for me to follow. When we were a little distance away, Maude confided, "I don't happen to think much of your friend. I just don't like her, but I may be wrong. Anyway, if she's any good, she'll smuggle in some phenobarbital tablets for me the next time she comes. Will you ask her?"

When I got back to the porch, Clara was very displeased. "What's the idea?" she complained. "I come to visit you, and you let me sit here while you go and talk to your nutty friends." I was offended, but Clara continued before I could cut in. "And by the way," she said, "don't ever introduce me to any of these crazy people around here again."

I was speechless. When I gained composure I said, "Clara, not all of these people are insane. There are drug addicts here and alcoholics like myself. You must remember, Clara, I'm here!" To my horror, Clara lifted her eyebrows and, with a toss to her chin, intoned, "Well?" I then poured forth a torrent of abuse—upbraiding Clara for her drunkenness and for her failure to do anything about my release. She left in blazing anger this time.

I was desperate to get out. I tried to think of people to whom I might appeal for help, but no one came to mind. Even if any of my friends had wanted to help me, they would not have been acceptable in the eyes of authorities.

Only reputable people were permitted to sign patients' release papers—people considered responsible and interested, concerned enough to oversee the patient's conduct and support upon release. Who among my disreputable friends would or could do this? As I searched my mind trying to think of someone who would help me, I remembered Raymond, my half-brother.

Both he and his wife were devout worshippers of God. Their reputations were without reproach and maybe they would care. As I thought of them, I recalled with remorse the many times I had laughed at them with scorn and mocked their faith. I had called them crazy religious fanatics. When they had asked me what I wanted from life, I had conceitedly said, "I want to travel and have plenty of money and live in the country's luxury hotels and be free to have fun." I had actually enjoyed seeing the shocked and disappointed look on their faces.

I thought of all this as I considered writing to Raymond and Lillian. I shrugged away all doubts about their willingness to forgive. As Christians, I reasoned, they *had* to forgive me if I asked, and I would ask. After all, I should certainly be willing to admit that they had chosen the right way of life and I had chosen the wrong one. "I'll tell them I'm sorry and that I want to live differently." I meant that, and started to compose the letter.

But another thought intruded—a dark one—almost as a voice whispering, "Don't do that! Don't write to your brother and his wife. They are fine, good-living Christian people. They will not want to soil their hands with anything like you. They will only laugh and agree that you are at last in the place where you belong. Why should they love you? What would make them want to go out of their way to help you after you have been so mean and unkind and caustic in your remarks about them? Don't give them the satisfaction of knowing where you are."

The apparent logic of these thoughts pandered to my pride and defeated my plan to appeal for my brother's help.

Every day was like the day before—except that with each day, my depression deepened and my despair increased. I fell to periods of morbid brooding. At last, my fevered brain fostered a plan of escape. I took it to Maude, expecting the fuel of her enthusiasm to feed the fires of my own desire for freedom. Maude listened with interest. When I had finished talking, she said, "Yes, it is good. It will work all right. There isn't much doubt that you can make it." But as she spoke, her typical enthusiasm was lacking. I was disappointed. Then she pitched in: "Jane, I'm an old-timer. I've been in and out of these places all my life. I know what it is to be hunted. Take a little advice from a woman old enough to be your mother. If you run away, if you get out the way you're planning, it will not be an escape—not really! You will always have that feeling of being hounded and hunted by the police. Jane, don't do it!"

I was both shocked and angered. This serious warning dampened my spirit, but did not quench my anger. "What do you mean, don't do it?" I railed. "If I don't get out this way, how will I ever leave this place? Who cares about me? Who will help me? If this plan isn't my escape, then what is?"

I kept repeating these last words over and over, demanding an answer. Maude looked hurt. This incident was probably one of the few times in her whole life Maude felt as a mother warning her young. She had almost never taken the role of counselor or adviser, and it was not easy for her to depart from her light, frivolous demeanor to do this. And now to be railed at for her pains. She just shrugged her shoulders and did not say another word.

Maude's passionate pleadings against my escape blasted hopes for that avenue of release. Her rush of words had been as rude cross marks canceling out a carefully wrought etching of my imagination. I lost heart. I lamented my circumstances, bitterly hating the doctors who had ordered my commitment.

Why had they committed me—why jail me? I had received no psychiatric treatment in the hospital. I had never been interviewed by a psychiatrist from the day I arrived. What was the therapeutic value of this hospitalization? I despised my sordid surroundings and felt outraged at what I believed to be the gross injustice of it all. Why should I have to face a possible lifetime of being caged in a loathsome place like this? I had met a number of patients, committed years ago as alcoholics, who remained in the institution simply because no one could be found to sign them out. I feared such a fate might be my own.

What had I ever done to deserve this? I had never hurt or harmed anyone, I reasoned. I had, by my drinking, hurt only myself, I thought, and it was not right to lock me up with psychopathic patients just because I had drunk a little too much whiskey. These were my self-deceptive thoughts.

I ate less and less of the soggy portions of tomatoes and bread served for lunch each day. Coffee, such as it was, had been my breakfast for weeks. At night, I found it increasingly difficult to cut the hunks of gristly meat on my plate with a spoon (our only eating implement). I ate little, did poor work in the laundry and spurned the "social life" of the ward.

An older woman saved a seat for me each evening, so I had at least a place to sit after standing at the ironing board all day. Not all patients had the luxury of a chair to sit on at the end of a day. She worked in the large sewing room, and it happened that her group was returned to the home ward a bit earlier than the laundry workers. I really appreciated the chair, but I so resented everything about the place that I found it difficult to express gratitude and thanks. Consequently this patient saw only my barely perceptible nod and the moving of my lips forming words that should have been said in clear, grateful tones. I rewarded her in no way—not even with a smile—for I was not wearing smiles these days, and my greetings amounted to grunts. Patients all around noticed my morose state, and some of the alcoholics sought to rouse me.

"You're not even trying," Maude scolded one day. "You're letting go. You can't allow yourself to do that." I did not have an answer. I just sat looking miserable. "Why don't you go to the dances?" Maude ventured to suggest.

I told Maude of my experience at the dance and of the first time I ever saw her, as she walked the length of the auditorium to the piano. "You say they clapped a long time?" she prodded. I could see she wanted me to tell more about the dramatic scene of her entrance. It was evidently an experience Maude enjoyed every week, and even the memory she found delightful. Maude was fond of herself, I concluded. But I still liked Maude.

Another time she suggested that I go to church. My look of impatient disdain disturbed her. She suspected that I was baffled over her suggestion and hastened to explain, "I'm not religious, you know. Not at all. It is just some place to go to take your mind off yourself and your troubles."

"Maude, save your breath!" I smiled. "I would be the last person in the world to suspect you of religious fervor." Oddly, this remark didn't have a reassuring effect. Maude frowned, offended: "I'm not exactly a heathen, either." She shot a sidelong glance at me, for she had been looking straight ahead into space as she talked. "No?" I questioned.

"No!—Well, I know there's something. You know—a power or something. But I don't believe in God."

Somehow, this morsel of thought had not sounded right. "I mean—that power or something is God," Maude rushed on, "but I don't believe in a God that punishes sin. What I mean is He or it is too big—what we do means nothing. This power has bigger matters to bother with. Anyway, no one knows if there is a God!" Then, since Maude could not seem to reinforce her defense with reason, she resorted to repetition. "Well, don't think I'm a heathen. I'm not a heathen." Thus the theological discourse came to an end.

I did line up with the patients one Sunday when the attendants called "Church!" I was taken to the Protestant service, where a preacher from one of the nearby churches volunteered a sermon. It was something about the penalty of using God's name in vain, and it bored me.

It was a habit with me that, when a public speaker was holding forth, I would listen to the speaker's first few words and decide, in the first two minutes of his address, whether I would listen to the rest of what he had to say or just close my mind and daydream. This preacher's monotonous drone and lifeless manner of delivery caused me to decide in a hurry in favor of the daydream routine, and even that degree of wakefulness suffered intrusions of slumber.

On our way to the home ward, I showed my contempt for the sermon with loud, hearty renderings of the preacher's forbidden words. It was a beautiful day and it was nice to get out, though it could not be said that walking four abreast with other patients was a leisurely stroll out in the open.

There came a time when nothing seemed to rouse me. What glimmer of hope had existed was either dead now, or dying. I could no longer feel a spark burning within. Thoughts began to trouble me—dark thoughts. Each dawn I awoke hating the gray intrusion to my slumber. Although sleep was fitful and there were many gaps of wakefulness during the night, I hated the day most of all and wished each morning that I could hit on some sudden, painless way of doing away with myself. I knew such thoughts could lead to the act, and I both desired and feared suicide. I was in just such a mood of total dejection one day when I heard my name being called. An attendant handed me a telegram. I opened it and read: "WIRE COL-LECT AND LET ME KNOW HOW YOU ARE." It was signed by my brother Raymond.

Chapter Eight

The telegram had been delayed in forwarding. Raymond had sent it to an old address where I had lived five years previous to my commitment to the state hospital. It was plain that he did not know where I was, but why had he sent this wire?

I knew I could not arrange with the hospital to wire my brother "collect" as he had proposed, for the authorities here would see no state of emergency. My reply would be in writing, and write I did.

I poured out my heart. "Raymond," I wrote, "How is it that just when I so desperately need someone to help me, you of your own accord, have wired to find out how I am? Well, I'll tell you, Raymond…" On and on, I wrote my thoughts as fast as they came, and paragraph followed paragraph. I told him I was sorry I had mocked him and Lillian for their faith. I confessed that I had been wrong. I further stated that if they would come to my rescue at this time, I would promise to live differently than I had ever lived before.

When I finished, I had to wipe tear splashes from the pages. There were no ink smears, as I did not have the luxury of a pen: I had written in pencil. Before I placed the thick letter to be censored and mailed, I held it in my hand and uttered something that sounded like a prayer. "Oh, God," I pleaded, "if there is a God, get me out of here!"

In spite of my cynical hardness of heart, I knew that receiving that telegram from my brother at this time was much more than a lucky break. I knew that it had something to do with the sign I saw in the little mission window the day my mother died: "MOTHER'S PRAYERS WILL FOLLOW."

I was thankful, and the tears that wet my cheeks now were not the scalding waters of remorse and bitterness that had burned my cheeks so often of late. They were tears of gratitude. To whom this gratitude was directed, I did not know. Somewhere, somehow, things were finally working out for me.

My exuberance splashed over on all, but only Maude Oberg was told the story behind my sudden joy. In a good-natured, friendly way, she shared my happiness without any taint of jealousy or envy over my good fortune. I found myself telling her much about my life. It was natural enough that she, in turn, told me something about herself. Not that her story had to be dragged out of her— Maude always waxed loquacious when the subject was "Maude." Egoism is usually frowned upon, but I felt no resentment toward Maude's frank and open self-interest; we are all interested in ourselves, I reasoned. Some of us think we are wise and clever enough to conceal it, for we seem to covet a reputation for modesty and humility— virtues foreign to most natures.

Maude told me she had been born and raised in upper Michigan—lumber country. Her mother had died in child-birth. An Indian couple, hearing what they thought to be the mewing of a kitten, traced the faint, whimpering cry under some bushes near their cabin. They found an infant wrapped in a potato sack. Maude's father, a gambler and drunkard, had deserted his baby daughter.

The Indians brought the baby to the nearby town, where a doctor who knew the foundling child's parents placed her with relatives of the mother. This family was large and they were ill-prepared to take care of even this tiny extra burden.

The Obergs, a kindly Swedish couple in Manistique, adopted the child, naming her Maude. Maude adored the gentle, loving woman who was her foster mother, and she respected her quiet, sober foster father. However, as she grew, she alarmed the townspeople with her high-spirited antics. They whispered unkind judgments and predic-tions. Yet, in spite of unwittingly offending the sensibilities of her elders and their consequent woeful prophecies, Maude's childhood was a happy one.

Her youthful playmates were less discriminating. They found, in the tall, genial redhead, a delightfully jolly leader with all kinds of unusual ideas for having fun. Thus Maude romped and played and grew under the bright smile and shining affection of the rather elderly Mrs. Oberg, who loved Maude as her very own.

A tutor was found to guide Maude's nimble fingers over piano keys—thus, it was discovered early that Maude had talent in music. Her tempestuous spirit calmed as she gave herself to musical instruction and practice, and she excelled. In Maude's fine talent, the Obergs had occasion to be thankful.

When finally the beloved Mother Oberg died and her foster father married again, pangs of loneliness sent tremors through Maude's being. She felt lost and unwanted.

Then she met Oscar, a young cub reporter for a Chicago newspaper, who was visiting relatives in Manistique. She fancied herself in love with him, and when he left town, she brooded. News soon came that Oscar had married. The spirited Maude took pains to cover her hurt.

After her foster mother's death, the townspeople—with the exception of a few girlfriends—rejected Maude completely. They didn't bother to hide the slights and snubs behind polite hypocrisies. She was rudely cast out of all social life. The gossip circulated was for the most part undeserved. Her nature was indeed suited to the temptations to which they imagined she had succumbed, but at this phase of her youth, Maude was guiltless.

Aware of their dislike for her, in a sort of perverted revenge, she purposely did things to startle and shock these people. In her unhappiness, she eventually asked her foster father and his new wife if she could go to the city to live. They gave her the money her real father had left for her in his will. He had, before he died, repented of deserting his child.

At fourteen years of age, Maude found herself in Chicago, very much on her own. She lied about her age to get jobs singing and playing piano in beer joints and bar-relhouses—also to get married. She was married and divorced before she was seventeen years of age. She became a well-known cabaret entertainer, and that is how she met the low characters with whom she later became involved.

Maude was married four times and legally divorced from only her first husband. When she was twenty-two years old, she stabbed and killed a man in self-defense during a drunken brawl. Maude faced the gallows for that act. But the appearance of a surprise witness the last day of the trial saved Maude's life.

She continued to drink and to carouse, and finally for a "new kick" tried dope. She became addicted and got into all kinds of rackets to get money to buy drugs. She finally had to peddle narcotics to keep up with this expensive habit.

Maude served time in city jails, county jails, work-houses, state prisons, and even in the Federal Penitentiary in Alderson, West Virginia. Her talent for singing and playing piano seemed to bring her to the notice of peo-ple—kind people who tried to help. She was given good jobs at times, but Maude never held them very long. She would do all right for a while, then off she would go on a spree and disappoint everybody. At last the drugs really got a stranglehold on her, and Maude was committed to the State Hospital in Kankakee as an addict.

"How awful to wind up here!" I said, thinking of Maude's age and the possibility that she might be con-fined in the institution for life, to which Maude laughed. "Oh, this isn't the first nuthouse I've been in. I was in Dunning with sleeping sickness. I slept my brains away for ten weeks. When I woke up, it was weeks before I could learn to walk or talk." Pointing, Maude said, "I'm blind in this eye from an overdose of drugs. I'm a mainliner, you know, and sometimes the stuff drove me crazy."

I felt very sorry for Maude. Now that a ray of hope was shining for me, I pitied her for her certain fate—to be caged in this place for the rest of her life.

An answer came from my brother to the letter I had written after his telegram arrived.

"Dear Jane," he wrote, "God's hand is upon you." His letter told how he was driving along the highway, certainly not thinking of me, when suddenly a voice spoke to him. It wasn't an audible voice, but the still small voice of the heart. "It was God," Raymond assured.

My eyes held to the words I was reading as though magnetized. His letter stated that God asked him to find out where his sister was. The Lord had said, "She needs your help and she needs it now!"

I had to put his letter down then. I could read no further for a while. I was crying, and some strange electrical feeling surged through my being. It was a glorious, exalted moment, unlike any other I had ever experienced. The nearest I had ever come to it was when I saw that sign in the little mission window the day my mother died, "MOTHER'S PRAYERS WILL FOLLOW." When I remembered that, more of these vibrations thrilled me. My heart seemed to bubble over with a strange new joy.

Yes! Yes! Raymond was right—THIS WAS GOD! I bowed my head and, for the first time in my life, I acknowledged within my heart that it was an unworthy head I was bowing—so unworthy of the blessings that were coming. "Oh God!" I said, "If You get me out of here, I will live differently than I've ever lived before. I want to thank You, God!"

My brother's letter further revealed that when the Lord spoke to him about me, he had not waited until he returned home to talk it over with Lillian. He had stopped in Wayne, Michigan, a little town he happened to be driving through, and sent a wire to the last address from which he had heard from me.

I was speechless! I marveled! I felt laughter going on inside of me—not the mirthless, cynical laughing to which I was accustomed, but a wonderful, new, thrilling joy! "How does one describe an experience like this?" I wondered. "I shall never, no never, be able to describe to people the way I feel right now," I said to myself. As I read the letter over again and again, I felt that joy bubbling in my heart. I cried and laughed and I knew—yes, I knew—it was God!

My brother and his wife exchanged a number of letters with me and also wrote to the superintendent of the Hospital. I knew that I would soon be called to staff, and I both feared and looked forward to that privilege. There would be about twenty doctors who would listen as I answered questions, after which their decision would be written to my brother. This procedure was necessary, of course, but it involved a lot of waiting, anxiety and worry, and I was not noted for having patience. This was going to be hard.

There were dark moments even after the arrival of that momentous telegram and the blessing of my brother's first letter. My faith had seemed boundless then, but now as I sat in the institution, waiting as the machinery of my release ground out its course, I became disgruntled. When they called me to staff, they would ask me what I thought of my being there. I had heard they always asked patients that. Well, I would tell them how I hated it and what a useless waste of time it was. I would point out that I never should have been put there in the first place, and that my release should be arranged speedily.

When my turn came, I had my rebuke firmly implanted in mind—even to the point of memorizing it.

Dr. Morrow opened the interview by asking the question I had anticipated—"How do you feel about being here?"

Contrary to my carefully premeditated answer and to my own utter astonishment, I found myself saying, "I have benefited by being here. Were I left at liberty to do as I wished, having no self control, I would have destroyed myself by drinking."

Heads nodded all along the table. After that, I just answered questions as thoughts came to my mind, and in almost every instance my answer was contrary to what I had planned. At the conclusion of that staff meeting, I knew by the manner of all doctors present and by the tone in Dr. Morrow's voice that I need not fear the outcome.

My next few days would not have to be spent in turmoil, worrying and doubting and wondering if my brother would be called to come and get me.

I had peace—and this peace I also knew was God. The mystery of why my answers were opposite to the answers I had planned was solved when I considered the matter afterwards. There could be no doubt—that, too, was GOD!

The much-hoped-for and long-awaited moment arrived when I was at last walking beside my brother and his wife to their car. We had left Ward 8-North, and Raymond hastened to open the car door. Before I got in, I took one backward glance. I wanted to look just once more at the drab building that had been my prison for the past three months. As I looked, I saw indeed what I had expected. Cold gray stones cruelly walled in their captives, and the black iron bars and heavy screening on the windows cast morbid shadows. Now I was seeing them from the outside, and that thought caused the brightening of my hopes for the future. My joy in entering into liberty was greatly intensified. I thought, "I'm no longer there! I'm out of that place now!"

I was about to turn away, satisfied, when I noticed the motion of a hand waving from one of the barred windows. Because of the thick screening I could not discern who was waving, but there was no mistaking the voice that called. It was the voice of "Angel Face." Maude Oberg was calling to me, "Oh, Jane, don't forget me! Come back and get me!"

Gone was Maude's usual gay tone—there was pathos in this call. I did not reflect a minute on how I would answer. I raised my hand high toward the window, more in the posture of an oath than a farewell wave, and I heard my voice saying, "I will, Maude! I'll come back some day and get you!" It was said with a conviction that surprised me. It was as though another voice had spoken—not my own.

Two minutes afterwards, seated in my brother's car, I regretted making the rash promise. We were on our way to Michigan, where I would be staying with Raymond and his wife Lillian until I found a job. My life would be very different from what it had been in the past, and the uncharted course I was to follow presented a challenge. Gnawing at my heart was a regret that I had so hastily promised Maude I would come back and get her.

Of course, I rationalized, she could not really expect me to do that. Certainly she would not be sitting back there pinning her hopes on an impulsive promise given at a highly exultant moment. She would know I had promised before I could reflect and consider how utterly impossible it was. Who could even dare imagine that I, an alcoholic patient with a record like mine, could take Maude Oberg, a woman with a record like hers, out of the State Hospital?

Maude would be bright enough to realize this—and would not depend on those hasty words uttered because—because—? I didn't know. Why had I made the promise? Oh, I wished I hadn't. Why did I have to spoil everything and look back at the ward building? Had I not done that, I would not have seen Maude's hand waving and perhaps I would not have heard her call. But that call! It was different. It was not like one voice, but like the voice of many. Yet I knew it was Maude's voice only. What had made it so different?

My brother and his wife, noticing my silence, started a bright and cheerful conversation as we drove along. I was grateful for their help and I wanted to be pleasing in every way, so I tried to sound interested in what they were saying by affecting a pleasant tone and eager manner when I made comments or answered questions. But my mind was on Maude, and when they finally asked about the poor soul who had called out the window, I was able to talk with genuine interest.

I told them all that Maude had told me about her life. They pitied her. I was surprised at their lack of condemnation. I had supposed that a religious frame of mind made one intolerant of the sins of others. I hoped, though, that they had not noticed or paid much attention to the words I had called back to Maude. If they had asked me how I expected to take Maude out of the institution, I would not have known what to say. I would have to admit that I knew it couldn't be done, and would find it confusing to try to explain why I had made that promise. Since I could not even explain it to myself, I dreaded the ordeal of trying to explain to anyone else. But I was spared. They did not say anything about this.

What was happening to me? Was a conscience at last being born within my soul? Things like this had never troubled me before, but nothing quite like this had ever happened until now. There seemed to be only one thing to do to save myself from feelings of remorse—I must forget the whole incident, just put it out of my mind entirely. I had intended to write to Maude and to one or two other patients in there, but I would have to abandon this plan altogether now. Since I could not find words to tell Maude why I had so rashly promised to do the impossible, I must forget about Maude Oberg completely and forever! That was settled. I leaned back in the car and looked out the window. I would relax and enjoy the ride as we drove through beautiful country to Rockwood, Michigan, my brother's home.

That night as I drifted off to sleep, I dreamed. I heard Maude Oberg calling again, "Oh, Jane! Don't forget me! Come back and get me!"

Now, at last free from my despairing bondage and with a sober mind, I could almost see myself as I truly was. The first defect I had to cope with was my lack of courage. I wanted to face life bravely and live uprightly—or I fancied that I wanted to—but I trembled at the prospect of fighting alone, without money and lacking presentable clothes, in a huge, strange, crowded city. If only I had a friend with whom to share this experience of pioneering in a new way of life. Of course, I had such a friend—Clara needed to change her way of living just as certainly as I needed to change mine.

Clara and I had been friends for nine years, during which the friendship failed to contribute in any way to its participants. Acquaintances dreaded our being together. We each seemed to bring out the worst in the other, they said. When we drank together, we quarreled and even fought physically at times. It got so that people hated to see us coming.

My father was less drastic in his denunciation of Clara than her folks were of me. Clara would be a good girl, they believed, if only she would stay away from Jane Page. My father preferred that we part company, but neither he nor anyone seemed able to separate us.

While I was in the psychopathic ward in Chicago, prior to being committed to Kankakee, Clara was questioned by a social worker.

"What is so wonderful about this friendship?" the woman asked when Clara had described it with that adjective.

"We have fun together," Clara returned. "We go places and—well, we get drunk together...."

"A wonderful friendship!" the social worker repeated

in agitation. "You get drunk together!" This summing-up made Clara angry, but she was stumped for incidents to offer that would enhance the social worker's impression of our friendship—or change anyone's opinion.

Clara De Runts

Chapter Nine

Clara was in Chicago now, about three hundred miles distant. And she was scheduled to remain there, too, for she had gotten into such trouble that she had been arrested and put on a year's probation. I was fairly certain that she would not break her probation and run away, but a plan was developing in my mind. I was not at all sure it would work, but it was worth a try.

The kind, compassionate attitude of my brother and his wife toward all unfortunate people gave me confidence to ask if they would take Clara into their home while she and I went job hunting together. They unhesitatingly consented. I omitted telling them about Clara's probation.

I promptly went to the telegraph office and wired, "COME AT ONCE. JOB WAITING."

Clara was working, waiting tables in a cheap hash house. When she received my wire, she did what I had hoped. She took the telegram to her probation officer and pleaded, "If you would allow me to take this job in Detroit, I would be away from my drinking friends. I could stay out of trouble and start a new life."

The probation officer was convinced. She gave Clara permission to come.

When Clara arrived I was at the bus depot to meet her. As soon as greetings were over, she came right to the point: "Jane, what kind of a job is waiting for me?" I was ready with an answer. I said,"Any kind at all, Clara. Take your pick." I handed her the help-wanted section of the newspaper. As she frowned, I said, "They are all waiting to be filled. All you need to do is to find the one job that is waiting for you."

As we pursued the tedious grind of job hunting, we were living at my brother's house in Rockwood, about twenty-five miles from Detroit. A neighbor who worked on the outskirts of the city drove us to the city limits each morning. From that point we walked or traveled by street-car to apply for jobs advertised in the newspapers. At the end of the day we again met this neighbor, who drove us back to Rockwood.

Each day was long and tiring. Clara had had some experience in waitress work, but she could give no local or recent references. I could not give references, and I lacked experience in any kind of work. I soon became very dis-couraged—Clara, too, was depressed. She faced having to write to her probation officer and report the location of the job that had reputedly been waiting for her. Whatever job she would get, she had planned to report as the one that had been waiting. But time was passing and neither of us had any job at all.

My brother and his wife were not financially prosperous. They were making time payments on their car, their little bungalow and their washing machine. Raymond drove an ambulance and Lillian worked as a nurse's helper in a large county hospital near Dearborn. Their salaries were not large, but their hearts were, and they unstintingly gave us shelter and food and daily carfare.

I felt guilty accepting this help. In the past, when I had money, I had never thought of sending them a little something to tide them over the hard times I knew they went through during the Depression. I had not even written!

I fell to wondering whether Clara and I could really make a go of our new life. Thoughts of easy money intruded into my thinking. Yes, I wanted to live a decent, honest life, I told myself, but I needed money to live on. I could go back to the rackets just long enough to get a few dollars ahead, and then I would quit. The money would enable us to go job hunting without worrying about things like carfare and cigarettes.

I was ashamed to make this suggestion to Clara. When she had come to Rockwood in response to my "job waiting" telegram, to dispel her disappointment concerning the lack of a job, I had talked with much conviction and confidence about living right. Clara had said, "It sounds good, Jane. I've never been at peace with myself living as I have, but the thing I question is the time. Is this the right time? Wouldn't it be better to go back in the rackets for a while, just to get a nest egg? We could quit as soon as we saved a few bucks."

I had vehemently objected, instead bravely proposing, "We will start with nothing and we will make the grade because God will see us trying and He will help."

Was that faith? Had I faith when I spoke these words to Clara? Well, if so, it was at a low ebb now. It was perhaps altogether gone. I felt torn inside. I wanted to believe that I really intended to do right, but…! At last I said aloud, "I might as well face the truth. I long to do right, but I just can't do it NOW!"

I feared going back into the life I despised—the life that had brought me nothing but sorrow, misery and suffering. The life that had brought me to the Kankakee State Hospital as an alcoholic. I had seen God's hand lift me out of there. I had promised the Lord I would live differently. What was I thinking? Was I actually planning to break my promise to HIM? No, I decided—no, I will not go back to my former life. I will go back to the institution instead!

In desperation, I went to Raymond. My words rushed at him.

"Raymond," I said, "what I am about to say may sound ungrateful. But I am not. I appreciate all you and Lillian have done for me and for Clara, too. But I'm not happy—I'm miserable. I thought that when I got out of the state hospital, I would be free. I know now that 'iron bars do not a prison make.' I am in a prison, an invisible prison, perhaps of my own making. I should be happy, but I'm not."

Raymond was about to speak, but I rushed on: "I have no desire to go back to the wretched life I lived before—I don't want to go back to it, but I'm afraid I will."

Then, seriously, I spoke the thought as it came to me: "Raymond, do you suppose I really belong in the state hospital, not as an alcoholic patient as everyone thought me, but as a mental case?"

I am not sure whether I expected him to be offended or angry or both. Instead, his serious features brightened into a smile.

"Jane, dear, your trouble is not anything a state hospital can remedy." He did not continue talking, but turned and called, "Lillian!"

He asked Lillian if there were a revival going on in any of the churches of the area. Lillian answered that churches were having their regular Sunday services and mid-week prayer meetings, but there had been no reports of the spirit of revival prevailing in any of them. I listened to all this, but did not know what they were talking about.

Lillian continued, "Friends write from Cincinnati that they are having real revival meetings in a tent."

"Let's get in the car and drive to Cincinnati," Raymond said. That seemed to settle everything. My conversation with him was apparently closed.

"Religious people are strange," I thought. "You start to talk to them about something, and they just smile and talk about something else." Of course, I should not have expected my brother to understand. He had never been in the humiliating position I was in now, having to accept charity and not having the nerve to ask for money for cigarettes, craving smokes as I was, worrying what I would do when my last pack ran out.

I took the pack from my pocket. It was about half full. I said to myself, or a silent voice said to me: "Jane, these are causing your dissatisfaction, are they not? You could accept the food and shelter without too much worry and you could accept the carfare, but you do not see how you are going to get along without cigarettes. Is that not so? Your fear of doing without smoking is driving you to consider returning to your old life, even to being committed again to Kankakee."

Unthinkable! But, nevertheless, I was thinking these thoughts and trying frantically to deny the self-accusation.

"Jane, you are addicted to cigarettes just as truly as you were addicted to alcohol."

I did not like that thought, either. Maybe I was being too hard on myself, I concluded. I would not want to ruin my entire life just for cigarettes! I would prove it to myself. I would take this last package and throw the few cigarettes that remained over the fence in the backyard. I had no money to buy more. I would quit them now—now while the urge was strongly upon me.

Clara was out in the yard, sitting under a shade tree, reading. When she saw me throw away my cigarettes, she asked, "What has happened? Has your brother forbidden you to smoke?"

Nervousness and regret were nagging me, for just the instant that my fingers had let the pack go as I tossed it over the fence, I fiercely craved a smoke. I managed to answer, "No, I have decided to quit."

Clara who never did have the habit and who smoked only rarely, was pleased. "I'm surprised you have the willpower," she said. "But it is a good time to quit, now that we're so broke."

Clara turned her back, changing her position to get under the shifting shade of the tree. A few minutes later, had she turned to look, she would have seen me standing at the fence again, peering with fiendish eyes, trying to see the cigarettes I had just tossed into the weeds. The weeds were high and there were thick bushes, and it was evident that I would have to climb the fence if I wanted to search for my cigarettes.

At the risk of being mocked by Clara if she caught me, I was nevertheless about to put my foot on the first fence rail when I heard Lillian's voice beside me. "Are you looking at our poison ivy?"

I was startled. I tried to think of some explanation for my being there. But Lillian was on her way. She called back, "Yes, there has been poison ivy growing in that spot for years." Her voice trailed off. "We should weed it out but it really isn't on our property and no one ever climbs the fence." My face was hot with shame and frustration.

Those cigarettes I tossed over the fence that day were the last I ever owned. I have never smoked since.

That afternoon, we all got into the car and Raymond drove us to Cincinnati, where a revival was in progress in a tent. I had never been in an atmosphere anything like this. Instead of a preacher doing the talking and everybody else sitting and silently listening, the preacher was speaking while everybody else was shouting pious expletives—"Glory to God!" "Praise the Lord!" "Hallelujah!" Some of them even jumped out of their seats and waved their hands in the air. Every face wore a bright glow. There were tears on many cheeks, not pouring from sad eyes but happy ones. I was as one transfixed.

The preacher's sermon was punctuated with these exclamations of blessing, but they were not interruptions, nor were they in the least disturbing. It all sounded like one great orchestra with various instruments playing just the right notes at the right time.

When I first entered, I stared in curiosity. Soon I began to look around at these joyous faces with admiration and even envy. Oh, if I too could come to feel as they did! But I was sure none of these people suffered my lot. No doubt everything in their lives was serene. But then, common sense made me doubt that. They had overcome.

I looked at my brother and his wife. They were not jumping around or doing any shouting. They were sitting there smiling and crying at the same time. Only Clara looked downright disgusted. But I quickly turned away from her and listened to what the preacher was saying.

His words shot out like blasts of fire—fire that could burn and destroy, but could also warm and brighten. I felt it working both ways in me. My sins and all my inclinations to sin were being seared by those fiery words. I could feel the pain of the burning. But I could also feel myself lighting up inside, and I felt warm and glad and hopeful. At last I heard the preacher say, "Those of you who have not the peace and joy of the Lord can receive Jesus Christ now. Will you raise your hands if you want to do this?" I noticed hands being raised.

In the brief moment it took to get to my feet, I rushed forward to get to the altar by the platform. I knelt there and prayed. "Dear God," I said, "I want to be like these people, and have the joy and peace they have. I know I have grievously sinned and I ask that You forgive me. My past is so terrible, and I am so weak I cannot promise anything, Lord. I can not even promise You that I will take another breath. You are the One who must give me the very next breath I take. I cannot promise to change my life, but You, dear Jesus, can change it for me. Come into my heart, Lord, and make me different."

What happened to me then beggars description. My whole being was flooded with a glorious new light and wonderful, transcendent joy. I couldn't contain it. I got up from my knees, faced the great audience and shouted, "Listen, everybody! I know! I know! I'm SAVED!"

That was all I could say. After that, I just stood there laughing and crying, too. Others ran to me—people I had never met embraced and kissed me. My brother and his wife were among them. They were still laughing and crying as they had been, but even more so now. Then I noticed that the altar was lined with others who had come forward and knelt as I had. There was much praising of the Lord going on. It was all real and wonderful—and I knew it would last FOREVER!

The salvation I received in my heart did last—but the joy was tempered when I walked to the back and saw Clara. She was livid. "Disgusting! This whole business makes me sick!" she spat. "And you up there with the rest, making a fool of yourself." It had been my habit to argue my point, but I caught my brother's smiling nod to let her alone.

This was something that could not be explained. No one could reason it out. It had to be experienced. My brother whispered to me later: "When you went up front to give your heart to the Lord, Clara said to me, 'Raymond, this is awful! The strain of drinking and being locked up and all Jane has gone through has finally affected her mind. Now look at her! She has completely lost her reason!'" Raymond and Lillian and I had a quiet chuckle over this.

104 / Chapter Nine

Clara sat sulking during the drive back to Rockwood. She said, "I should have known your mind was slipping when I saw you toss those cigarettes over the fence."

I said simply, "I'll admit I lost my own mind, Clara, but I've found the mind of Christ."

When she said, "What kind of gibberish is that?" I did not try to answer.

Chapter Ten

Clara and I soon left my brother's home to live and work in Detroit. We rented a little back bedroom with a gas plate on Cass Avenue and Henry Street for four dollars a week. I bought primary colors in tempera paint and some lettering brushes. I planned to make a living writing show cards for retail merchants of our neighborhood.

I would have to solicit my own orders, so I worked on a sample book of layouts: "HEELS WHILE YOU WAIT," "HAMBURGERS 10¢" "DRESS SALE," and other card signs suitable to the local stores. As I took my sample lettering from door to door, restaurant managers, shoe repair shops, millinery salons, beauty parlors, dry goods stores and the like gave me orders and I was kept busy.

As it turned out, I was extremely busy earning very little money. My hands were still shaking from my past bout with alcohol and I rounded O's and crossed T's with strenuous effort to acquire steadiness. I was very slow in turning out work. I could not seem to accumulate enough money to invest in supplies for my little sign business. When I did succeed in soliciting work, I had to walk about twenty-four blocks to and from the art supply store to buy the particular material needed for each order. All that added to the time it took to earn my living.

In addition to the hurdles presented by the business of soliciting sign orders, making repeated trips to the art store buying limited supplies, painting signs and delivering them, I had jolts and disappointments with some of my customers, too.

I well remember the first time I was given an order for a ten-foot banner. It consisted of three lines of reading matter and I accepted the order gladly. At the art supply store I bought a heavy roll of sign paper a yard wide. This could not be purchased in measured lengths; they sold it only by the roll. After toting it over a mile and a half to our little rented room on Cass Avenue, I was confronted with the problem of how I was going to do the lettering.

Measuring and cutting ten feet from the roll was the least of my problems. After I had cut the needed length, I despaired as to how I would fasten it to the wall to do the lettering. I would use thumbtacks, of course, but in our little room ten feet of wall space was not available. The wall length was interrupted by a window on one side and a door on the other. I considered turning the corner of the room with my paper, but decided against it. I knew I couldn't space my lettering correctly that way.

With Clara helping me, we hit on what we thought was a solution. We would spread the sign paper the full length of the wall, and when we came to the corner we would simply roll the paper and tack it there, to wait until I painted the spread-out section. When that was finished and dry, then it could be rolled and the unfinished end of the banner could be unrolled and painted.

Now, this process called for some skilled measuring, which I thought I was prepared to do.

"Let's see—in my first line I had thirteen letters to paint." Allowing four inches of margin on both sides of the banner, and an inch between letters, and allowing a full space between the two words, I would have, I figured, a seven-inch limit for every letter.

As I did this job letter by letter, via the yardstick-spacing method, it all looked very well. But when I finished the banner and removed it from the wall, unrolling both ends the full length of the floor—there was something mighty odd looking about it. All the letters were in perfect shape, I was sure of that—and yet they didn't look right somehow. My tall, narrow 7" x 12" *M* was squeezed into the same seven-inch width that the letter *I* had to be spread out to fill.

Clara, who liked to encourage me whenever possible, had to be frank: "The letters are shaped right," she said, "but something is wrong."

"Well, I've checked over my measurements, and no mistakes have been made. It has to be right," I concluded, hastily adding, "You will deliver it for me, won't you?"

Clara looked as if she was going to cry, but she choked back whatever objection she was about to voice and nodded consent.

We walked together to Michigan Avenue where the sign was to be delivered. "I'll wait here," I said to Clara. "I'm new at this and I'm a little shy at delivering my own work." Clara's nod told me she understood.

I was waiting across Michigan Avenue, which was quite a wide street, and my view of Clara and the proprietor of the shoe repair shop was indistinct through the plate-glass window. It appeared as though they were both standing looking down at the floor. I guessed the banner had probably been laid out there. For what seemed to be endless time, they both stood there. I became tired of standing on one foot and then the other, and began to pace short distances back and forth on the street corner.

At last, I saw Clara coming out the door without the banner! I felt ashamed to pray about such a trivial matter as this, but I had prayed, and now I thanked the Lord in my heart. When she crossed the street and we were face-to-face, I started. "Did he—?"

Clara cut in. "Yes, he took it and he paid me, but I was pretty embarrassed." She told me the bitter truth.

"He spread the banner on the floor," she said, "and he stared at it. He scratched his head, then stood and stared some more. He would look at me and then back at the banner—then scratch his head. All this time he said nothing and I said nothing.

"Then, suddenly, he quickly went to the cash register and got the money and handed it to me. I promptly thanked him and left. I was afraid to ask what was wrong. I thought the less said, the better."

I blushed. My pride was hurt and yet I knew (as Clara knew, and no doubt the customer knew) there was something wrong with that sign. Yet, at the time I'm sure that none of us knew exactly what was wrong.

The next night, I suggested to Clara, "Let's take a walk down Woodward to Michigan Avenue and take another look at that sign. Maybe it will look different when we see it up in the window."

We walked, but we didn't see. The sign wasn't there.

"Well, maybe he just didn't get a chance to put it up yet."

The following night, we walked again to Michigan Avenue. Still no sign. The next night we again made our pilgrimage—but no sign of the sign.

After a while we abandoned our nightly trudge and walked there once a week, each time hoping the proprietor had at last found time to put up that sign. It occurred to us—but we didn't wish to admit the thought—the man was not even trying to find time to put up that banner! I had no way of knowing that fifty years later, I would be wondering how that sign might have looked in that man's window!

Clara finally got a job as "soda jerk" at a soda fountain in a drugstore at a salary of ten dollars a week, and at last she was able to report to her probation officer. Between the two of us, we were barely able to pay rent, buy food, manage my paint supplies and Clara's uniforms, and buy a few pieces of direly needed clothing. We were glad to be rid of the vices of our former way of living, but missed comforts and even some necessities.

Clara was not exactly sharing my attitude of religious fervor, but she was very pleased with what she boasted as her self-reform. She was proud that she had found within herself the ability to resist temptation, sever affiliations with former friends and depart completely from her old way of living. She was not drinking and was now working honestly. When she was a small child, her mother had trained her in a religion, so Clara had a religion, too. She was quite satisfied.

Clara was born on the outskirts of Chicago back in 1909. She was so tiny at birth they kept her warm in a coffeepot. Her father's two marriages had brought twenty-one children into the world. His present wife, Clara's mother, was a hard-working woman. She said her beads, sent her children off to church, but was too busy to do more. Heavy family washings, the shoveling of coal and snow, darning, mending, cooking, ironing—these tasks filled her days and drained her energy.

So when little Sophie, Albert, Rose, Sammie, Clara—any of them—came to Mommie for a hug, she would busily shoo them away: "Be off with you!"

Clara's father labored doing landscape work for others and farmed for himself. There were short times of prosperity for the family, after which they would be plunged into the most abject poverty, to remain thus for years.

Nick De Runtz would not read contracts, deeds or leases, and was indifferent about getting receipts for the money he paid out. He willed to trust people, and those he trusted lied and cheated and stole from him. Nick drank strong liquor and taught his offspring to drink. He made his children work hard. They were sent out into the fields to bend their backs and dig into the earth. In her teens, Clara worked in a nearby can factory. She took other jobs, too, many kinds, waitress work among them.

It was at a time when she was out of work that she met me. She thought me very smart when I quipped, "Clara, work is made for horses and even they turn their backs to it." What is worse, she accepted this doggerel as pure philosophy.

After we teamed up, there were times when we really thought ourselves prosperous. Our wardrobes were piled with every type of outfit from evening dresses to riding habits. We had the latest and the best-made cars, and plenty of money to throw around in bars. A certain class of people admired and respected us for being "smart." Some even envied us, but we wound up drinking and dissipating, and in the process spent our money and lost everything. Our health suffered and the pain and disgrace of poverty became our lot, too. Now, after seeing the shallowness, and suffering the aftermath of this kind of life, Clara was happy in her reformed state. And quite proud.

I knew this was not the real thing, either. I wanted my friend to know the joy that I knew and to experience the deep, wonderful peace that possessed my own soul. I talked constantly about the Lord and His way and persuaded Clara to attend church meetings with me where the gospel of Jesus Christ was preached. She was docile as far as attending these meetings was concerned, but when the invitation was given to accept Christ, Clara would sit rigid.

I tried to prod her to a decision. I would say, "Clara dear, why don't you give your heart to the Lord?" She was always angry when I asked her to do that. She would say in irritation, "Jane! You must stop that! I told you I was in a religion different from yours. I'm all right. I'm not doing anything wrong. What is the matter with me?" I would urge, "But you need to be saved, Clara." "Saved? What is that?"

I would explain that she needed salvation from her sins. In furious anger, Clara would bark out proclamations of her good living and present reformed life. In white rage she would say, "I'm no sinner! You stop calling me that! I'm not sinning!"

I feared I had made the wrong approach and I prayed for guidance in dealing with Clara. I decided to be tactful and employ gentleness. Clara heard about God from morning until night in every manner of conversation. I could always find a way to mention HIM, to bring God's name into everything. Finally, as we were having breakfast one morning, Clara dropped her spoon on the table with a bang.

"This has got to stop. I get God served with my dish of oatmeal. At noon, He's in my bowl of soup. At night, I find Him in my pillowcase." (I had begun stuffing tracts in Clara's purse, in her pockets, and under her pillow.) "This has got to stop!" she wailed.

I could see the girl was really suffering. I had not wanted her miserable—I only wanted to see her truly converted.

Perhaps I had better seek the advice of someone, I decided in desperation. I sought the counsel of an evangelist who was holding meetings in a nearby church. I had not selected churches with any denominational preference—I went where they preached about Jesus Christ and His love. The evangelist, Merven Rosell, smiled even when I almost cried as I told him how badly I wanted Clara to be saved. But he was not being rude; my zeal without knowledge amused him.

"I talk to her about the Lord morning, noon and night," I said breathlessly, "but she will not listen. She even resents this."

I was surprised when he said, "Why, of course she does. You are talking too much."

That stunned me. He went on to tell me that I should not talk to Clara about religious matters any more. "You have already said everything. Keep still now and give it time to sink in."

He saw that I was not accepting this. Even though this man was famous for his evangelism, I was not going to allow anyone to forbid me to talk about God. My spine was stiffening self-righteously when suddenly the logic of it all came shining through.

"Will you promise me you will stop talking to your friend until she comes and asks questions? She will, you know. And when she does, don't give her overdoses. Be careful to answer briefly and to the point."

I saw what he meant now and agreed, but even as I did, I allowed myself one reservation. The tracts—the gospel tracts! He said nothing about them.

I did not know that Clara had, that very morning, prayed on her way to work, "Oh, God, stop that girl from talking to me about religion!" She did not have much faith that her prayer would be answered, and so she decided to spare herself some preaching by having her hours changed. If she worked nights, she would not be free to accompany me to evening church services. As she found my nagging insistence hard to resist, she usually gave in. She was quite happy to tell me about this new work schedule, but did not disclose that she had asked for the change.

Clara thought she was getting a break at last. All of a sudden I had ceased to annoy her with pleadings to become converted, and I had even stopped injecting God into every conversation. When she got to work the first night of her new shift, she basked in the thought she would be spared hearing a sermon, when lo! She was hearing one.

The manager had turned on the radio to a gospel preaching message—one that was shouted in emphasis, too. Clara sighed, "I will not listen to the words." But she listened and she heard and she resented everything. Finally, when this ironic turn of fate tormented her to the extent she could bear it no longer, she went to the manager and said, "You are a Jew. You don't believe any of that stuff you listen to over the radio. Why do you turn it on?" His face reddened. It was not Clara's place to question him and order his selection of radio programs. He shrugged his shoulders and replied, "I like the man's voice." That was all and he did not change the station.

I kept my promise to the evangelist who had advised me. I did not speak to Clara about the Lord. But every once in a while I would know, by Clara's cursing under her breath and the sound of paper being crushed, that she had found another gospel tract. In her pockets, in her shoes, always under her pillow—everywhere I could think of, I put them. This was my way of speaking these days.

Chapter Eleven

From the time I left Kankakee, I had determined to put Maude Oberg out of my mind. It would be necessary for me to forget her plight if I myself wanted to be happy. But she came to mind very often, always in the same way.

In the morning when I woke, I would hear, "Jane, don't forget me! Come back and get me!" I would hear that call at noonday when I walked the streets soliciting sign orders. I heard her call for help many nights as I went to bed, and even during sleep I heard the call.

Why this memory to torment me? I owed Maude Oberg nothing. I had made a hasty promise, but I had asked God to forgive me for that, along with the other sins for which I needed forgiveness. As I thus reasoned, the thought occurred that I had not made one single effort to impart to Maude Oberg the light that I was now enjoying.

I should at least write to her and explain the way of salvation. Yes, I should and I would.

When I told Clara of my intention, she was adamant. "Now, Jane, we've quit the former life. We have quit all our old friends. Let us leave the past alone. We don't want to drag some old dope fiend back into our lives now. I am going to ask you to do this one thing for me, for friendship's sake. Promise me you will not write to Maude Oberg."

I found it hard to make that promise, but Clara was desperate. And there was logic to what she said. If I dragged old friends back into our lives, she might be tempted to do the same. At last I agreed—"I promise that I will not write unless some day you change your mind." Finally, that frightened me. I did not want Maude Oberg to die unsaved. But now I had made a promise. I was a Christian, and I knew I must keep my word. Well, I could pray for Maude.

With my sample case under my arm, I would walk miles along Woodward Avenue soliciting all manner of merchants for sign orders. The cement sidewalks were hard and unyielding to tired feet, and the tall buildings a bit austere. Facades of granite, marble, brick, and steel towered ominously to dwarf the size and importance of one treading their paved canyons.

The shopkeepers were usually receptive to what I had to show. A number of them looked with interest at my samples and placed orders on the spot. Some viewed my work favorably and took my business card, promising to call when they needed my services. The telephone number printed on the card was that of the landlady of our rooming house, who was kind enough to call me when customers placed orders.

Very rarely was anyone gruff or rude. Door-to-door soliciting is hard work at best, but the Lord had removed the sting from this weary trudge by directing my way among pleasant people.

I was trying hard and really putting my best into each job of sign-writing I did. Whenever I came short through lack of knowledge or technique, the Lord covered my mistakes—or made a way, somehow, for the acceptance of my work.

One time an order came in from a drugstore for some illustrations of ice cream sundaes to be displayed at the soda fountain. I enjoyed doing the artwork, sketching transparent glass dishes with scoops of ice cream of different hues, depicting chocolate, vanilla, strawberry, etc., and lettering each label.

Clara had been at work during the time I was painting these little poster cards, and when she came home, I had them all placed around our room for her immediate view. When she looked at these pictures and read their labels, she frowned.

"Jane, they're pretty, but they are not going to be accepted!"

She hastened to explain why. "They do not serve sundaes in dishes of that shape. Not in any soda fountain where I ever worked."

I was bewildered. What to do now?

Clara said, "Let me take them in. I have to shop for groceries down that way and we might as well learn the worst in a hurry."

"All that work and material wasted," was all I could think.

In about an hour, Clara returned from her combination shopping and sign-delivery trip. She had a bag of groceries but no sign cards. I thought she could have at least brought them back. She didn't have to toss them in the gutter! They were not too clumsy to carry.

But she was smiling and my heart began to lift.

"Jane, the most wonderful and unusual thing happened, " she said as she placed the groceries on the table. "The manager of the drug store wanted to telephone, but he mislaid your card. He couldn't find your number in the directory, of course. He wanted to reach you so that he could describe the new dishes he had just ordered in which to serve his ice cream sundaes. When I delivered your posters, he was amazed.

"'How did Miss Page know?' he asked.

"I of course said, 'Know what?'

"Then he told me all about the new dishes and how he tried to get in touch with you! And Jane—would you believe it? The dishes you painted are the exact shape of the ones he is going to use!"

Like sailors who take boat rides on their days off, Clara, the waitress, and I, the door-to-door sign saleswoman, found recreation in walking. In the evening hours, we would walk through and around a square block of parkway nearby, and perhaps sit on a bench for a while if the weather was warm. Simple refreshments, such as candy bars and popsicles, satisfied us.

Or we would walk along Woodward Avenue, viewing window displays. In this way I gleaned ideas for show-cards and posters. These shop windows were my only classrooms where I could study and learn my trade.

Sometimes, we would walk miles to a store displaying my signs and showcards in the window. Clara shared my enjoyment of this limited measure of success.

We began to prosper a little. Clara got a small raise at the drugstore and also made a few dollars each week in tips. I was acquiring a little more speed in my sign-writing and made enough money to stock a few supplies. My trips to the art supply store did not have to be made so frequently.

I had faithfully attended services in three different churches, and in all of them I heard about tithing. Tithing, it was explained, was an Old Testament law given to the Israelites, but the principle still held good for the support of God's work. Clara and I were pooling our money, and it did not occur to me that she would object when I proposed we tithe. But object she did!

Clara was a thin little person with snappy brown eyes and a small, pleasant, heart-shaped face, but she could scowl at times—and this was one of the times. She shouted, "I know *you* are batty on religion, but *I'm* not, see? If you want to give your hard-earned money to the churches, go ahead, but not a penny of mine will go there!"

I had to accept this. After all, Clara had the right to do what she wanted with her own money. As for me, however, I put one-tenth of my earnings in offering baskets. Clara sneered but did not try to talk me out of this notion. My little business began to increase.

One day I pointed out to Clara, "God has been blessing me and it is because I am tithing. If the Lord sends me in twenty dollars worth of work this week, I am going to give Him twenty percent instead of just ten percent of my earnings."

Clara did not try to restrain her anger and disgust. "You overdo everything," she said. "It is bad enough to give what you are already giving, but to give more yet! A dime in any offering plate is plenty. That is all I ever intend to give."

I wanted so much to say, "But this is giving to the Lord, Clara, not just the church."

A day or two after that conversation, Clara unexpectedly returned to our little room shortly after she had left for work. She was happy. "I'll have to hurry to my job, Jane, or I'll be late," she said, "but I did want to bring this order to you. As I was crossing the street, a car stopped. Mrs. Abrams, who has that dress shop on Woodward Avenue, recognized me as your friend. She had a sign order all written out and gave it to me so that you could get started on it right away."

I hurriedly took the sheets from Clara's hands and started to figure. "Clara!" I exclaimed jubilantly. "This is about thirty dollars worth of work. Now I can give the Lord that twenty percent I promised Him."

Late or not late, Clara didn't leave then. Not until she upbraided me—"Jane, what do you mean? You said you would give God twenty percent if He sent you an order for twenty dollars. Well, God did not send it. Can't you see? I brought it in. Not God—*ME*!"

This last, she fairly screamed.

The day came when I suggested that we purchase an automobile. Some of my showcards and posters were large and bulky and hard to deliver by streetcar or bus. I needed transportation. Clara went along with the idea.

We went to a used-car lot where rows of long, sleek hoods flashed their polished surfaces like a color chart for enamel paint. Shiny chrome grillwork sparked their toothy grins, the circular headlights staring at us as we walked along and looked.

The salesman at our elbow furnished background music for this march, singing the praises of each vehicle we passed. "Now, *here's* a clean little job."

"Let's tell him what we're able to pay, "Clara whispered.

"Have you got anything real cheap?" I asked bluntly. He didn't like the word and he hedged, so I hit on another way of asking the same question. "Do you have something serviceable and yet very inexpensive?" We followed him to a row in the back of the lot.

I nudged Clara: "This must be 'death row'." There, all the retired vehicles of over a decade were slumped—a row of battered and bent metal, rusting on wheels. The salesman kicked the smooth tires of one old Ford that somehow looked less lame than the others. "This one runs," is all he said. "You can drive it away for fifty dollars."

After starting the motor and satisfying ourselves that it was indeed the thing for us, we asked if twenty dollars would be enough to pay down. The salesman just laughed at our little joke. But we weren't laughing. We were waiting for his answer. It took a moment for him to register that we were serious.

"Wait here," he said.

When he came back, he announced, "Yes, we will take

your twenty dollars. Could you pay ten dollars a month until the car is paid for?" We thought it time to ask about financing charges. Very obligingly, the salesman waved the problem aside. "This deal isn't going through the bank, girls. We're going to trust you to make the payments directly to us. There will be no finance charges."

After the signing of papers and the paying of our twenty dollars, we had one more question for the unsuspecting salesman. "How about gasoline—is there gas in the car now?"

We were told there was probably enough to turn the motor over a couple of times. "She will need gas, but you can get it right on the corner. You can take her away now."

Clara and I looked at each other. We would have to come back. We explained that we—er—didn't happen to have much money with us right now.

The amazed gentleman then did a most amazing thing. He drove the car to the nearby gas station and filled it. "With the compliments of the Dealer!" he smiled, as he held the door open with a low bow.

The car ran, but it sort of spurted and jumped at times—most times, in fact, and so we named it "Leaping." It did a splendid job of delivery work for my card signs and posters, though. We were well satisfied.

It had been a great effort to stop talking to Clara about her soul, but I managed to keep my word to the evangelist. The tracts I habitually slipped into Clara's pockets and under her pillow did my talking for me as long as she read them. But lately I noticed that Clara was not reading them.

The moment she saw one, she would angrily destroy it without glancing at its contents. This disturbed me. The evangelist had said that if I kept still, Clara would soon be asking questions. When would this be? It seemed she took her respite quite joyfully, and even curiosity had not moved her to ask why I had stopped nagging—lest her asking would start me off again, I supposed.

One night I was sitting in our room, working late on a sign order to meet an early morning deadline. Clara was turning in early. I noticed her walk out in the hall with a tract I had just placed under her pillow.

I peeked through the door. She was reading every word of it.

"Thank God," I breathed.

When she came in, I looked at her face to see if the tract's message had gotten through. I wished I had not looked. I saw bitterness there.

"Religion!" she snarled, "So this is religion!" Clara was raising her voice. "Religion is supposed to make you feel peaceful and good inside—not miserable and discouraged like this tract makes me feel!"

I felt sorry for her but I could honestly think of no comforting words.

"This tract says that all sinners shall be cast into hell!"

I could still think of nothing to say. Tears began to come to Clara's eyes. She said, "That is not a nice thought to go to bed on!"

I stood, staring. I wanted to offer comfort, but words stuck in my throat.

In the morning, I thought it best not to revive the subject and so I started a conversation about the weather or some triviality. But Clara was frowning.

Her next words revealed that she was not thinking of the upsetting tract of the night before. "Jane," she said, "I had a dream last night."

"I dreamed that I was sewing, trying to patch an old piece of cloth, and each time I put in a new piece, the old piece would tear. I was doing that all night in my sleep. Isn't that funny?"

No diplomacy held me in check now. I was not thinking of tact. I was thinking of only one thing—where in the Bible had I read that? I had read it, I was sure, but was not familiar enough with the Book to be able to find this particular Scripture now. I wanted to tell Clara that her dream was in the Bible, but I was sure she would not believe it unless I could show it to her in print. How could I ever hope to find it in this vital moment?

I reached for my Bible and flipped it open at random. I might as well start looking from anywhere my eyes happened to fall. My eyes read and my lips moved, as aloud I read to Clara on the very page I had opened to, "No man putteth a piece of new cloth unto an old garment, for that which is put in to fill it up taketh from the garment, and the rent is made worse" (Matt. 9:16).

Clara was not angry. "Tell me what it means," she asked, wide-eyed.

"It means, Clara, that putting a new piece of cloth in an old garment is like trying to patch up the old life. It doesn't work. Self-reform is a patch job. Let God make your whole life new by surrendering your all to Him."

This time I had not spoken. God had spoken through His Word, and Clara received it.

Chapter Twelve

Since the manager of the drug store had the habit of tuning the radio to a gospel preaching program every night, Clara was pleased when her working hours were changed back to the day shift. I was quick to fill her free evenings with evangelistic services in nearby churches. As Clara's resistance was low, my insistent invitations were successful. As the proverbial lamb, she went where her pride in self-reform was indeed slaughtered. Those who preached sounded out against self-effort and good works as a means of Salvation. Salvation was by faith alone, they said.

Satisfied that Clara was getting God's message, I was silent at home. Then she asked questions, as the evangelist had said she would. "Why do these crazy preachers say that people should not do good to get to heaven?" I told her that no one could ever do enough good to deserve heaven; that eternal life is a free gift from the Savior. After having received eternal life through faith in God, the believer naturally wants to do things that are good and right—not to earn salvation, but in gratitude for salvation. She shook her head and looked puzzled.

An outburst of rebellion came from Clara one night as we walked home from a service: "This friendship is asking too much. I have a different religion and I don't want to hear the things they say in those churches you take me to. I'm not going again."

I went alone after that. Each night, I was able to find something going on in at least one of the three churches I attended. I had stopped begging Clara to be saved. She had spurned my deluge of gospel tracts. Now, she flatly refused to attend meetings. What was left?

I could pray, of course, and I did. But I had to ask, "Clara, will you tell me what it is about the services you don't like?" Her look said I should not have asked. "Don't you know they are a bore?" she replied. "I can endure sitting through a dull meeting. Somehow I can manage that, but the worst part is the way a person feels when the service is over." I was not following. "They all say the same thing at the very end," she explained. I still did not understand. Clara then told me, "All those preachers ask for sinners to be saved at the close of each service."

"What is wrong with that?" I wanted to know. She amazed me as she said curtly, "I don't know. We will just leave it there. I don't know why, but that part makes me nervous."

Some weeks later, a young Italian evangelist came to Detroit from Brooklyn, New York. Joe Morone was different. With fire and native wit, he dared to inject slang phrases to denounce sin and to exalt God. He spoke boldly with a pronounced Brooklyn accent. I knew instantly that Clara would like him.

But how to get her to go? That was the question. I had used all my persuasive powers, my stubborn and persistent demands, and even my sweet and subtle pleadings. There remained no new tricks to pull out of the bag. I could only plead with her to come just once more as I prayed that God would move her heart. My prayer was answered. She said yes.

During the service I could see her interest mounting. Evidently she was fascinated by this young preacher's manner of delivery.

At the end of the service he, too, did what Clara had objected to—he asked all sinners to come forward to the altar and accept Christ. "Oh, Lord, don't let this spoil it for Clara," I prayed.

When we left, she was smiling pleasantly. Without any prodding from me, she chirped, "I like him." I remembered that his message, though seasoned with slang, was sound, and that his invitation to sinners was not unlike the others to whom Clara had objected so strongly. Timidly and not without a tremor of fear, I reminded her that this man, too, had asked sinners to come forward. Clara's manner was entirely changed. "Oh, that! I don't mind that anymore. I will go with you again tomorrow night."

I should have been content to let well enough alone and be thankful for this turn of events, but I just had to ask, "Why doesn't the invitation to sinners bother you any more?" She answered brightly, "It never should have bothered me in the first place. I don't know why it ever did. As I've thought the matter through, that invitation is not for me. I am not a sinner."

It was all I could do to keep my mouth shut then, but I prayed hard and God helped me do it.

Clara promised to go with me to the service again the next night, but added that it would be the last. I should have considered this a victory. I had begged her to attend only once more and she had, of her own accord, volunteered to attend a second night. But Clara was such a hard case. I needed many more nights, many more services, much more talking and convincing. But I seemed to be barred from every avenue of approach, and now my chance to win her to Christ was narrowed down to just one more service. I was very glum until my heart heard a whisper: "Do you doubt that God can save her in that one service?"

No, of course not. I knew the Lord could reach her heart in this last service, and I prayed (with more hope than faith) that He would.

That night, Joe Morone preached on why Jesus went to the cross to redeem a lost world. He talked about those who were self-righteous and who felt that their own personal goodness was enough to win for themselves heaven's glory. Joe backed up everything he said with Scripture and showed that no one who ever lived was perfect enough to merit eternal life. No one was righteous enough to stand faultless and flawless in the presence of a Holy God. God's holiness demands only purity that could be fulfilled in none other than His Son, Jesus Christ. And those who believe in Christ, His righteousness is imputed.

At the end of his sermon, Joe asked a few questions:

"Those of you in this meeting tonight who think that by your own good works you can earn your way to heaven, answer me this—if you could do this, then why did Christ have to go to Calvary and suffer and bleed and die to purchase your redemption? If you, by a few good deeds—doing the best you can—if you could earn salvation that way, then why did Christ pay the price for your redemption at such an agonizing cost?"

Before Joe began the final invitation to sinners to accept Christ, he asked one more question, "Do you think that God would have sacrificed His Son needlessly?"

The service was finished, the usual invitation given, and we were walking home. I saw only the sidewalk as I kept my head lowered to hide my tears. The last service was over, and Clara was not saved! Clara was silent. I was thankful for that. I felt too discouraged to clash with her in an argument, and my heart was too heavy for light banter.

When we closed the door of our little hall bedroom, I thought my heart would break. In another minute I would surely have burst out in sobs. Suddenly, Clara broke the silence and asked, "Can I give my life to God right here in this room, now?"

I would have given anything at that moment to be able to say all the fine and brilliant things I had heard others preach in sermons, but I just stood there feeling limp, and when I spoke, I blubbered. My stammering tongue tasted salty tears. It was Clara who gently took my elbow and pulled me to my knees beside her.

At the bedside she prayed:

"Dear God, that preacher said we don't have to be in a church in order to talk to God; that we can come to Jesus anywhere we are and be saved. Even now, in this little room, I can ask You to come into my heart.

"I always thought that coming to God meant going to church. But now I see there is a difference. Church can't save, but Christ can. I must look above and beyond the limits of any church building or denomination. I must look up much higher—up to heaven where the Lord is.

"I'm looking up now and I'm asking for forgiveness for my sins. You said in Your Word that if I asked, You would answer. I'm going to thank You now, dear God, because I know You've heard me. Thank You, Jesus, for my salvation."

I had been holding my breath as I knelt beside her, listening—afraid that the sound of my own breathing would disturb the solemn moment. And I, who longed to be so helpful, slumped weak and useless across the bed and wept.

Chapter Thirteen

First, Clara wrote to her probation officer. She confessed the deception about the job waiting in Detroit and told of her conversion to Christ. I knew that Clara had made a complete surrender to the Lord, for her manner of speech changed, her thinking was different and her face was aglow. We enjoyed a new fellowship and a close companionship. We prayed together, read God's Word, bowed our heads in thanks at mealtime and enjoyed attending gospel services.

The one window in our little room on Cass Avenue faced a brick wall. There was a tree growing in the little patch of yard below, and its branches were silhouetted in a network of dark lines against the sunlit brick background. The sun brought out tints of every color in those clay bricks, and through the etched branches, the effect was gorgeous. With my tempera sign colors, I painted this simple scene.

I think to this day it is one of the best paintings I have ever done, and later it received the esteem of competent art scholars. But Clara wouldn't let me sell it or give it to anyone.

"It is your new way of seeing things," she said. "It is your new vision—your new life, really!"

Such simple little pleasures added zest to our days. We were past needing excitement and swirling activity to keep us from boredom.

In our building on the same floor where we rented, a young couple lived in the large room up front. Meeting them in the hallway and on the steps from time to time, we became acquainted. Ray was out of work, taking odd jobs by the day or by the hour to make ends meet. His young wife, Ada, was pregnant, expecting her baby in a few weeks.

With our old car, "Leaping," we were able to drive Ada to the clinic for her checkups, and once in a while we found the means to offer other little aids and services. When it came Ada's time to deliver, our old "Leaping" delivered first. We drove Ada to the hospital, where a very tiny and sweet little baby girl was born.

Of course, in our association with these two we had testified to them about the Lord, but we told them nothing about ourselves. We succeeded only in impressing them that we were "religious," and were unable to persuade them to accompany us to church. They liked us, however, and were friendly and seemed very grateful for our few favors.

In my persistent solicitation for sign orders, I finally got an order from another shoe repairman. It was to read: "WE REPAIR WEDGED HEELS."

I say "another" shoe repairman, because the "banner-man" on Michigan Avenue, who didn't hang his sign, had had a shoe repair shop. Some strange quirk in my thinking had convinced me that shoe repairmen were hard to please. I determined to make a beauty of a sign for this customer. I not only did the lettering carefully and neatly, but I added for good measure an unasked-for illustration: I painted two feminine feet shod in wedged-heel shoes, and nearby I pictured a little black Scottie dog.

I didn't ask Clara to deliver this. I proudly presented it to my customer personally. He frowned. "I didn't order anything like that." I hurried to assure him that I was not adding to the price I had quoted. "That makes no difference," he grumbled. "I don't want that sign. It is not what I ordered. I ordered a plain two-by-three feet oilcloth sign reading, 'We Repair Wedged Heels.' That is what I ordered, and I'll not pay for anything else."

This time, I was really crushed. At home, all Clara's efforts to cheer and encourage me failed. "I guess I'm just no good as a sign painter," I sighed despairingly.

Suddenly, Clara's face brightened. "Jane, I've got it! This sign is your wedge! It's your wedge, Jane," she enthused. "This sign is not like that banner. There was surely something wrong with that, we know. But this is really very nice work. You and I are going to take that out and use it as a sample. We will solicit other shoe repair shops with it and get orders for more."

Incredible? But something went "click" inside me at Clara's suggestion. And that is just what we did, and that is just what happened. I had order upon order for duplicates of that sample sign we carried around. It was indeed my wedge! Had the irate customer accepted it, I never would have made anything near to what I profited because he rejected it. I thanked the Lord for the windfall He provided through this incident.

Not long after Clara's conversion, she came to me and said, "I have been thinking about Maude Oberg. She has a soul. I didn't like her and I still do not think much of dope fiends, but you should write and tell her about salvation."

I wrote pages and pages, then showed them to Clara before putting them in the mail. Clara's approval was evident as she smiled and nodded, her eyes scanning the words. Suddenly, she scowled. "Oh, Jane, you must leave this part out. It is all right to tell Maude about the Lord and to say we will pray for her, but don't tell her we are going to try to help her. How can we do that?"

My faith had reached a new high, and I said joyfully, "God will make a way to take Maude here with us."

She handed the letter back, expecting me to make the suggested omissions, but I did not reply nor did I change the letter before I mailed it.

At the state hospital, Maude read the letter twice, but still could not understand it. The third time she read it through, she decided she knew what we were trying to say. To the other patients circled around her, Maude explained, "This letter is in code. Not code, exactly, but it is meant for me to read between the lines. These girls, Jane and Clara, are in Detroit now and they have a new racket. I'm sure that is what is meant by this sentence: 'We have found something wonderful—better than anything we have ever had before.'"

The alcoholics to whom Maude was reading nodded in agreement. Maude further explained, "These two are smart. They have written in this way so the doctors here or anyone in authority will not know what is meant if the letter should fall into their hands."

Everybody was admiring the cleverness of Clara and Jane. Maude offered a further interpretation: "From what I can make out, they are in some kind of a religious racket."

She frowned. "That will be new to me. I've never been in a religious racket before." Proudly, she told her listeners, "They must think I'm a smart old bag, for they want me in it, too. Listen to this: 'And Maude dear, we want you to share what we have found.'"

There were smiles and nods.

And we were pleased too, when we got Maude's reply. She wrote in a large scrawl, saying she was glad for us—good luck—and she would be waiting to hear how she could fit into all this.

She was sure that we too, would read between the lines of her letter just as she had read between the lines of ours. But we saw only the words she had written, and they meant to us only what they said. We concluded that Maude had apparently accepted our testimonies and was anxious to know what God could do for her.

Chapter Fourteen

I had written several times to my father, and at last I got a message from him. He had had a stroke and was in a convalescent home in Chicago. He would be so happy if we could come to see him.

Making "car" payments for "Leaping," we had even less money than formerly, and our clothes were getting to look quite shabby. Mine didn't fit anymore, as I had begun to gain weight. My coat did not close in front. I hoped that people who saw me with my coat open in cold weather would think I was one of those fresh-air fiends who love chill breezes blowing on throat and chest. Our shoes needed mending, too. We were able to afford the shoe repair job, but the clothes had to do. We would eat less and save money for the trip to Chicago. Clara and I wanted to see my father and her mother, and I was determined to see Maude.

Bread and peanut butter was inexpensive and filling— and for me, it was fattening, too. We had toast in the morning, bread and peanut butter for lunch, and bread and peanut butter for dinner. On Sundays, Clara made Spanish rice or some hamburger dish.

In planning our first Thanksgiving day together since we had been saved, Clara and I decided to "let ourselves go" financially, and have turkey and all the trimmings. There was an oven under our two-burners, and Clara planned to cook the turkey and make dressing, etc. We had allowed ourselves but meager fare for months now, and we really looked forward to our day of joyous feasting on Thanksgiving.

Thanksgiving morning, my brother knocked on the door of our little all-purpose room and told us his car was downstairs. We were to get our coats on and go to his home for the day. We wanted to appear grateful, for we were pleased with this invitation, but we longed to spend the day as we had planned.

"We would go, Raymond," I said, "but we can't. We've bought a small turkey and were about to put it in the oven now."

He smiled. "Well, Lillian and I have counted on that. We thought you would be having turkey, and so I thought this would be the right time to pick you up and bring you and your turkey over to the house where Lillian will cook it and serve it to all of us."

We were a bit amazed, but we agreed and hastily packed our turkey for transportation. At my brother's home, he led the way, loudly proclaiming, "They had a turkey, Lillian, just as we had hoped, so now you can get busy and cook dinner."

Clara offered to help in the kitchen and I offered to set the table, but we were ushered into the modest living room and told to sit there until dinner was ready. Lillian wanted to do all the cooking herself. She said she wanted no one bothering her in the kitchen.

We sank into the saggy but comfortable overstuffed chairs and prepared for a long visit with Raymond. It would take Lillian hours to cook that turkey and prepare and serve dinner all by herself.

But presto! In a few minutes the table was set—and in came the turkey, all cooked deliciously brown and ready to eat. We noticed it had grown in proportions, too. It was much larger than the small bird we had bought. Then we caught on. Lillian had everything almost ready by the time Raymond arrived with us, and it took but a few minutes to set the table and bring on the food.

Oh, we had a wonderful time that day. The food was perfect, and the joy of being together and praising the Lord was thrilling. When we left that evening to return to our room in Detroit, we had with us our little turkey entirely intact, all cooked and stuffed and with lots of trimmings added. Lillian had expertly prepared it for us in her fine oven after we had feasted on their turkey—not ours.

Thanksgiving feasting lasted through that day, and in our little room in Detroit, it lasted through the next day and even the next. We did not tire of eating the same kind of food three days in a row, for we had long denied ourselves such feasts. Speaking of how long this dinner lasted—the truth is it lasted much, much longer than the next day and the day after that. It is well over fifty years now, and it has lasted in memories of blessing until now and will perhaps last evermore, for that dinner was not confined to the consumption of physical food, as the love that supplied that dinner consisted of food for the soul.

~

Clara's heart had softened to the extent that she thought Maude Oberg should be told the way of salvation, but when I even hinted that we might help Maude, she hardened. "We must keep the past out of our minds and above all, out of our lives," she insisted.

We had been getting along so well that I feared to put on too much pressure and spoil the sweet fellowship and harmony we now enjoyed. But I had not omitted from my letter to Maude the particular parts to which Clara had objected. I was desperate to win Clara to my way of thinking before we faced Maude when we visited Kankakee. I was squelched every time I mentioned the subject. This time, I decided God would have to work without me. I didn't see how the Lord was going to do it, but as I had been defeated in every effort, I had to drop the matter. I prayed about it daily, however, while we saved our pennies for the planned trip.

One day, Clara brought home a sparkling bit of luxury. She had purchased some bath salts. The beautiful box had caught her eye. I never had a particular skill for economy, but now that we were denying ourselves to save for this trip, I was displeased. I considered this an extravagance we could have done without. However, I did not voice my disappointment. I thought, "Well, now that we have it, I might as well use some in my bathwater tonight."

Clara saw me starting to unwrap the cellophane. "Don't! Don't do that!" she called.

I stopped.

"I bought that especially for Maude. When she comes to live with us, she will like some nice little thing to brighten her dresser."

Checked by Divine Wisdom from saying words that rushed to my mind, like "When did you change, Clara?" I stammered "Oh, yes," instead.

"Leaping's" windshield got a good wiping, and we even rubbed down the old bent tin of her ragged fenders and the corrugated hood. She was not beautiful, but she was clean and she ran. As we drove to Chicago, oil fumes coming through the floorboards stifled us, but we chugged along.

My father actually cried when we arrived. He was speechless for a while. We did the talking. I had told him in my letters all about the Lord and now Clara and I both described our new way of life. He listened and I noticed he was not resenting this. But his mind was not weighing religious doctrines right then. He was very happy to see his daughter again.

"All my life I had Raymond all wrong," he confessed. "I never thought he had it in him to do the wonderful thing he did for you."

We talked of my release; of Raymond and Lillian's kindness; of our work and of our church attendance. Most of all, we talked about the Lord.

Several times during this conversation, my dad acted as though he wanted to break in and say something. He would make the effort, then stop short. Finally, he told us: "Jane and Clara, I have always denied God. When you wrote of your new-found faith, I contented myself that it was the lesser of two evils. Religion was false, but alcohol was harmful. I remember I told you once that it would not last. I believed that.

"One night in my rooming house, a phone call came for me. The voice over the phone said my daughter was in the County Hospital, dying. When I questioned, they said she had been drinking. A car hit her. I told them my daughter was not in Chicago. She was in Detroit and had quit drinking, but I found myself saying all this into a buzzing receiver. I had an awful moment then. I remembered how I had insisted that your God wasn't real. Now I found myself wishing that the whole thing had been real.

"At the hospital, they ushered me to a bedside where I looked down at a young woman who was a stranger to me. There was a screen around her bed, and I knew what that meant. She was just regaining consciousness. I sat on the chair, my knees weak from the emotional strain. I was going to sit there for a minute until I had the strength to get up and leave. They had made a mistake, and I was so glad—so very glad!

"Then this poor girl's voice came weakly, 'Mr. Page, I know you.' She talked in a very small voice and spoke her words slowly. She was one of Jane's friends; one of the friends who used to drink with Jane.

"'You never liked me, Mr. Page,' she said. I gave her hand a squeeze and said I was sorry to see her here in this condition. I did not remember her at all. She said they must have found Jane's name and my address in her purse and thought she was Jane. I agreed that, yes, that must be the way the mistake had been made. Then, without thinking, I said aloud, 'I'm so glad it wasn't Jane!' Then I apologized for saying that. The whole thing was awkward. The girl looked up at me and said, 'I know, Mr. Page, that I am dying.'

"'I'm an atheist,' I said, 'and I can't give you any hope about God and the hereafter. I'm sorry.' She looked away. I felt pity for the poor girl. I said, 'I can tell you about Jane. Do you want to hear about her?' She nodded.

"I told her all about you, Jane. I told her how you wrote and said that Jesus Christ saved your soul and changed your life. At the end, I found a stirring going on in my own breast and I finished by saying, 'And it IS real.' My pity returned and I sought to apologize again for my lack. I said to the girl, 'I'm sorry I can't offer any help at all.' She didn't answer and her head was turned away, and so I got up and started to leave. I heard her voice coming a little stronger. She was calling to me. 'Mr. Page, you have helped me. If Jesus can do that for Jane—He can help me, too!'"

When my father had finished telling us this, my heart lifted to God in thanksgiving. I knew that my father was not far from the Kingdom of God. "Save him soon, Lord," I silently prayed.

In my father's emotional state, he had failed to get the girl's name, but I knew who she was, and felt God's assurance concerning her soul.

We had budgeted our finances carefully to make this trip, and stayed overnight with friends of my father. We did not look up any of our own former friends. We saw Clara's mother and had a nice visit with her. When we left Chicago the next day, we drove eighty-five miles to Kankakee to see Maude Oberg.

Maude's greeting was warm and we enjoyed talking. It was also nice to greet other patients I had known there.

Clara and I had managed from our meager budget the price of a New Testament for Maude and some candy. She accepted this gratefully, but looked puzzled. I tried to explain about the promise I had made a year ago, to take her out of the institution, and Maude shrugged. "Don't you think I knew it was impossible?"

"But things are different now," I said with enthusiasm. "Our lives have been changed, and I am going to ask Dr. Morrow today if they will release you to us."

Maude said, "Uh-huh."

I began my talk with Dr. Morrow by telling about God's grace in transforming my life. He listened with respectful interest. Then I asked outright for Maude Oberg's release. He said, "You're not serious?"

Clara assured him that we were.

"Have you any idea of what her record in crime is like?" he asked. "She's no kid, you know. What could you do to change Maude Oberg?"

Almost in chorus we said, "We can't change Maude, but the God that changed us can do the same for her and we believe He will."

Dr. Morrow pushed a button and his secretary appeared. He asked for Maude's and my records from the files. Clara and I sat there watching him read from one record and then from the other. He would finish a few lines from papers in his right hand, then shake his head and turn to read from papers in his left hand. Frowning, he questioned, "Do you think this state hospital would release a woman like Maude Oberg, with an entire life of crime, to you who also have a bad record?"

Clara spoke up. "Jane is not the person you are read-ing about from those papers. Christ has made her new!"

This kindly doctor who superintended this large insti-tution spoke gently. "I do respect your changed lives and I am really glad for you. I wish to encourage you all I can, but my advice is to go back to Detroit and forget Maude Oberg. Go on living in the wonderful new way you have been telling me about."

We looked at him. What he read in our eyes caused him to say: "All right. I'll do this much for you. I know it can't succeed, so don't pin your hopes on it. But I will pre-sent Maude Oberg before the staff and tell them you have asked for her release."

We were thrilled and were about to pour forth thanks.

"Wait a minute!" he said. "I will not recommend this. I can't. But I will bring her case before the staff just to make you happy."

It *did* make us happy. We left Kankakee that day rejoic-ing as we scooted along in the dented vehicle that was "Leaping." And no royal personages ever felt as regally transported as we did on our ride back to Detroit. God had blessed us with wings of faith.

Back home again in Detroit, we sat in our little hall bedroom and talked about old times—certainly not with any longing to live again as we had before, but with gen-uine appreciation for the way God had changed our lives. The past offered no lure to us. If anything, looking back on the pit from whence God lifted us made our new life in

Christ shine in brighter contrast. We could see, too, why all the evil forces that beat upon our lives could not break this friendship.

God had a plan for it.

At present, we did not have in our wardrobe hangers loaded with lovely frocks and evening gowns; no new sleek automobile of the latest model stood outside our house. There was no money in the bank, or in our purses, either. We were not renting a hotel suite with maid service and dining out in lavish style with charming male escorts.

We had a small table and a few tin plates and cups, and big square slices of bread with peanut butter, and oh, such contentment! And we had such joy that at times we thought our very hearts would burst.

I would wonder at times why it seemed to be my lot to labor hours over sign-cards and banners bearing such mundane messages as the cost of haircuts and the price of spaghetti dinners. I longed to shout my knowledge of salvation from the housetops and tell others what I was learning about God and His ways. I wanted to shake the earth, and here I was merely shaking a limp reed in the marketplace.

I was in such a meditative mood one day when I received an order from a nearby gallery. The manager called on the telephone asking that I send someone to pick up his copy. Clara brought back a picture of a bearded gentleman under which I was to letter the man's name preceded by the title: "Worshipful Master." It was probably a dignitary of some lodge or secret order, but I rebelled at the thought of such a title conferred upon a mere man. I sent

Clara back with the picture and the message: "There is only One worthy to be called 'Worshipful Master' and He is the God whom I truly worship enough to reserve that manner of address for none other than the Lord Jesus Christ."

Clara told him that as she announced my refusal to letter the picture. He accepted my message with a tolerant smile and urged her to ask me to come and see him personally. I wasn't going to go at first, but I reasoned that even though he probably wanted to argue over the personage in the picture and his right to the title of honor, I would at least have an opportunity to testify about the Lord. "It may be that God is opening to me this door of witness," I thought.

The manager greeted me warmly. He not only extended his hand, but also bowed respectfully and expressed his pleasure that I had come. He proceeded immediately to escort me through his galleries. There were exquisite oil paintings of great value, and before each one he paused, asking two questions: "Do you like this one? Could you do such work as this, Miss Page?"

I answered in the affirmative each time to the first question, for the paintings were truly lovely. To the second question, I had to answer in the negative, of course. I could not approach such talent. But after the first dozen or so pictures, I became a little irritated. Viewing the paintings could have been a pleasure, but the questions were annoyingly repetitious. Didn't he know by this time that I did not consider myself in the category of those artists?

However, he kept that up until every picture was seen, at which point we had made the rounds and were standing by his front door again. Then abruptly, and with much less courtesy than that with which he had received me, he opened the door and bowed me out. "That will be all, Miss Page. Thank you for coming."

I found myself stammering in embarrassment. Maybe I said "thank you" or "goodbye"—I don't remember exactly. But I was thinking, "I've not been given a chance to say anything other than repeating over and over the same answers to his same two questions. I have failed to testify about the Lord." But what was I to do? I had not expected anything like this.

I wondered, of course, what it was all about. I never did see that man again, and so I was never told what his purpose was, but I ventured a guess. Apparently, he wished to diminish me. Since I had, in my refusal to letter the picture, reduced his revered personage to that of mere man, he was attempting to make me feel inferior by forcing my repeated confessions of lack of ability in art. I was made to see that, even in my chosen work, I was most inferior.

Perhaps I should have laughed it off, but the arrow of humiliation had penetrated as I reflected on my lack compared to these master painters. I questioned God about this.

Yes, it is true. In my chosen work—in that ability in which I seem to excel—I am less than the least. Why is this? No doubt those artists were all unbelievers. The biographies of such geniuses reveal they are, for the most part, a godless lot. And yet God—the giver of all gifts—had endowed them with talent as far above mine as the heavens are above the earth. I felt this was unjust. Why was not I, a believer, given at least equal ability with the infidels? I would certainly use my talent to the glory of the Lord. But I did not have such talent. Why?

I fell to brooding, so much so that when I was given a sign order announcing to a few whiskered pedestrians who would walk by Joe's barber shop that Joe was including a shave with the price of a haircut, I rebelled. The idea that my fingers, my mind, my energies must engage in such crude and inconsequential messages, instead of the profound message upon my heart, generated anger. I said aloud one day, "I hate my brushes!"

I was made aware that God heard me. Of course, I knew He read the thoughts and intents of my heart before utterance was made, but as I spoke voicing my displeasure, a feeling of guilt swept over me. I realized that I had been criticizing God's leading and provision for me.

I tried to shake this off. "God must see that I am preferring His service to these material things," I reasoned. But as the days passed and no sign orders came in, and even when I went out to solicit orders, I couldn't get any—I realized the Lord's displeasure over my expressed hatred for the measure of talent He had graciously given me. I was on the verge of repenting, but I didn't repent. In my heart I still loathed the prospect of going back to painting signs about Joe's haircuts and the like.

Days dragged into weeks. Three weeks' rent unpaid and still no sign orders! In desperation, Clara and I searched the want ads. For some months now, Clara had not been working for hire. She had been working with me full time, delivering my sign orders and doing other helpful tasks incidental to my sign business. We depended on this for our living.

Clara expressed her wonder: "What has happened to your sign business? I just can't understand this." I said nothing. I knew all too well what had happened and why.

We were accepted for employment at a huge, famous brand bakery, and were placed on benches beside a belt that transported cookies. We, among other packers, were to snatch these cookies from the transporting belt and place them in boxes. We were instructed as to the exact manner in which these cookies were to be picked up at a certain required speed. Remember, this was back in the '40s. I'm sure this process has long been replaced with high-tech methods.

I was placed at the very end of this belt, where a huge disposal bin received the crumbs and broken cookies that remained on the belt after the packers had finished. I was responsible to capture all cookies that remained whole before they fell into the disposal bin with the broken pieces.

If any of the packers slowed down a bit, I had to work "on the double" to catch the cookies before they fell. Being new and not especially gifted in assembly-line techniques, I slipped up a few times and lost some whole cookies. A piercing cry from the supervisor could be heard above the din of the machinery on such occasions. When I turned to apologize or explain, she thrust her arm out as in a Hitler salute and pointed to the belt. "Don't stop! Look, you're losing more cookies!"

Clara was not used to standing on her feet such long hours, and neither was I. Clara had to leave her bench twice with nosebleeds. My feet hurt plenty, but otherwise I made the long hours of our first shift.

In the dressing room, as we were putting on our things to go home, the young girls, strong and hardy, shouted to each other, "Are you going dancing tonight, Nancy?" "No, tonight is my bowling night!"

How could they? What kind of feet did they have? Mine were like boils. Clara's feet bothered her, but not to the extent mine pained. I could hardly walk. I limped to the streetcar and managed to hobble up the flight of stairs to our apartment. When I sank into a chair, I moaned, "Oh, Lord, forgive me. I love my brushes and want to use them again."

I picked up my Bible to find solace, and behold! As I read—or tried to—I found that the print traveled off the pages and spilled over the side just as the cookies had done all day long. The print wouldn't stand still. I could not read a word.

I knew that Clara could not stand the job, and I was aware that my feet wouldn't take it. Even my heart was pounding—and now my eyes, playing tricks with traveling print! I prayed again:

"Dear Lord, send me an order—any kind of order. I will not complain. I will do it and be thankful."

In a matter of minutes, I was called to the phone. It was one of my sign customers. A shoe store wanted me to come over right away and pick up the copy. This time I did not send Clara as I usually did, but hobbled over on my feet, which felt like two boils. There was quite a good order ready for me. As I stuffed the several sheets into my purse, the store manager came forward with a foot-square cardboard sign. He said, "Here, take this along and make a dozen just like it for our other stores." I looked. It read: "DO YOUR FEET HURT?"

Maude Oberg

Chapter Fifteen

As we talked of helping Maude, we summed up what we had to offer. In our building we could rent another little hall bedroom. This one would be cheaper, because it need not have a gas plate. Maude could have her coffee with us and eat what we cooked in our room. These would be the necessities of life, but there would be more—there would be LIFE, as Maude had never known it and as we had just come to know it. God would prosper us, but we would not worry about material things since we had everything—*everything*!—EVERYTHING!—in the way of joy and peace and blessing!

It was thrilling to plan for Maude, but at times I wondered if we had a right to. I voiced this doubt to Clara.

"We have a debt to Raymond and Lillian," I reminded. "They took me out of that place and kept me while I looked for work and they helped you, too, Clara."

"Yes," she agreed. "We must pay them back before we can help anyone."

In Rockwood that Sunday we enjoyed another of Lillian's good dinners. It was nice to be visiting in their home again and we loved being with them. They laughed at "Leaping" in a sweet, good-natured way. We laughed with them, but this hurt a little, too, for we had come to respect "Leaping" as the car that God had given us. As bent and beat-up as she was, she came into our lives legitimately, which is more than could be vouched for her shiny, high-powered predecessors. We loved the old thing.

Before we left, we told Raymond and Lillian that we guessed it was time for us to begin paying them a little on what we owed. For an answer, they just exchanged glances and smiled. We pressed on. "You must have kept account of it all. Let us know how much it is and we will pay something each week."

Raymond said, "Yes, Lillian kept account. Go and get the list, Lillian."

While she was looking for the list, he asked what had become of Maude Oberg. I said, "Oh, we've testified to Maude and we plan to help her some day. We want to take her out of that place."

Lillian returned with the list and read it. It was higher than we had imagined. When she finished reading, Raymond said, "This is entirely cancelled. You owe us nothing."

We tried to insist—we were sincere, too. Raymond and Lillian would have it no other way. It was their gift to the

Lord, they said. Raymond smiled, "Now you are free of debt. You can afford to help Maude."

Driving the few miles from Rockwood back to Detroit, my joy was quenched by another responsibility coming to mind—a responsibility I had toward my own father. We had seen him in Chicago managing on old-age pension and living in a convalescent home. It was my place as his daughter to minister to him. I should do that, I thought, before I entertained ideas about helping a comparative stranger I had met in a state hospital. I told this to Clara.

She did not agree. "Your father is better off where he is. He is provided for and given better care than you would be able to give. You would be doing him an injustice if you were to insist upon doing something you are not capable of."

Clara, however, left the matter for me to decide. "It is your problem and your father. Do as you see fit."

I wrote to my father, telling him of our plans to take Maude with us. But I pointed out that I knew my first responsibility was toward him. I would put all thoughts of Maude out of my mind and concentrate on making a home for him if he said so.

I got an immediate answer.

"Forget about me. I am all right here. Do what you can for Maude Oberg. Remember, I have lived my life and am almost at the end. Maude has a few years ahead of her."

"Leaping" was beginning to give us a little trouble. She had carried on bravely, bearing her scars of wear and tear with only slight grunts and rumblings, but now she began to roar her need for attention. Instead of stockings, a new fan belt had to be purchased, and instead of a blouse, a set of spark plugs. We had clutch trouble, and the threadbare tires were threatening to come to an explosive end any day now.

Our plans of philanthropy began to appear ridiculous. Here we were, planning to take Maude out of the institution, and we really had nothing to give. She might even be ashamed of us. Our clothes were getting shabbier every day. We hadn't been able to afford larger living quarters and were cramped for space for my sign painting materials. And now this threatened collapse of transportation would curtail possible income from bulky poster jobs that depended on the car for delivery.

We knew that Lillian and Raymond thought experiences such as we were then going through made people stronger and developed character, and so we were not surprised that they had not offered to help. Nor did we want to ask them, or anyone for that matter. But we began to doubt that we should plan on an extra responsibility—an extra burden—in the person of Maude.

As I thought along these lines, the idea came that we need not altogether abandon our plan to help Maude. We could just postpone our help until we were really on our feet. We should have a nice apartment to share and good food on the table and plenty of it, presentable clothes to wear, and even a fairly decent late-model car. All this might take a couple of years or so, but then we would be in a position to really help her. Now we were not even meeting our own needs, it seemed.

Then God spoke to me. We were made to see that if we wouldn't help someone on our way up, we wouldn't help

anyone once we got up: "There will always be a good reason not to."

I told Clara these thoughts and this answer. She admitted that she, too, had been wondering, and that God had
shown the answer to both of us.

The very day our finances were completely depleted, a
letter came from my father. We were always glad to hear
from him. His letters of late had taken on a tone bordering
on faith, and he always expressed happiness over Clara
and me.

This time as I opened the envelope, a twenty-dollar bill
tumbled out. What was this? His letter explained that for
some strange reason—he didn't know why—he felt compelled to save some money and send it to us. His cash
allowance was very limited, but he had cut down on his
tobacco to save the enclosed. He trusted we could make
good use of it.

The next day, we got another letter. When I saw the post-
mark, my hands trembled opening it. The letter was from
Kankakee, Illinois, and was signed by Dr. Morrow. In formal
wording, we were advised that Maude Oberg would be
released to us. Would we come for her the following week?

At that instant, Clara and I knew the strange reason
my father had felt compelled to save his tobacco money in
order to send it to us. He would someday rejoice, knowing
that his sacrifice paid our way to Kankakee to get Maude
out of her dungeon.

Careful budgeting would be required for this trip, and
so instead of wiring a reply to Kankakee, we wrote our

answer and mailed it within the hour. Yes! Praise God! We would be there!

We saw our landlady and asked if there were another small bedroom that we could rent. She showed us a room without a door. All that separated it from the public hall was a curtain. An unfrosted electric light bulb dangled from the ceiling, and the furnishings included a chair and a swayback bed. Maude would need a bureau, but we could put an orange crate in there with a little mirror on top and the pretty box of bath salts Clara had long been saving for the occasion. We took the room. It cost two dollars a week.

I said, "Clara, our expenses are getting high."

"We must have faith," she sighed.

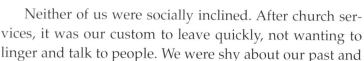

Neither of us were socially inclined. After church services, it was our custom to leave quickly, not wanting to linger and talk to people. We were shy about our past and ashamed of our clothes, too. In spite of our reticence, some of the members sought us out. They always greeted us, making every effort to make us feel welcome.

At this time we felt the need to talk. We wanted to see how other Christians would accept Maude, and so we told some pleasant people we met in church about Maude and our plans to help her.

Their faces changed as they listened. They did not spare us. "There is a zeal without knowledge," they scolded. "You two young women are new converts. You should spend years reading and studying the Bible before you set yourselves up as counselors of others. The woman you describe is unlikely to accept salvation. At her age, people seldom do. Her way of life is too deeply ingrained. You are not only endangering your own spiritual welfare, but you are doing society an injustice by thrusting upon it one whose villainous acts have brought her under lock and key, where she should in all justice remain. If she is to be converted, you can visit her there and preach to her, and she can accept salvation right where she is. It will not hurt her to stay there, but it would be very dangerous for all concerned for you to take her out."

In the same way that someone thrown from a horse wants to get back on and ride again, so as not to lose nerve, we went immediately and confided to two other people—a married couple who had known my mother years ago. Edith and Marion's response was heartwarming: "If God is in this, He will not only assure your hearts but He will also bring it to pass."

That night, Clara and I knelt side by side at the little bed upon which we slept and at which we knelt the night Clara accepted the Lord. We remembered what dear Edith and Marion had said.

Chapter Sixteen

"Leaping" was definitely not cooperating. Here we were on the highway to Kankakee to get Maude, with very little money to manage on, and "Leaping" was chugging and spurting and even stalling at times.

Finally, we had to pull into a garage. When the mechanic's head emerged from under the hood, he had bad news. The job would take several hours. He had repair work lined up and would not be able to get to it until the next day. The cost would be twenty-five dollars.

Seeing the dying look on our faces, he asked, "What's the matter? Can't you stay over until tomorrow?" We promptly told him no, we couldn't wait and also that we could not afford to pay twenty-five dollars for the repair. We just did not have the money.

The young man scratched his head. "I only work here," he said. "I can't do the work any sooner, nor can I reduce the cost, but I know a fellow who needs work. He's had a few troubles and he will take a job like this, and I think he will give you a break."

We thanked him and followed his directions to the fellow's house.

We soon found the place and were told that although the job was worth twenty-five dollars anywhere else, he would take seven dollars. "Okay?" he intoned. It was certainly okay, although it was painfully unaffordable—sort of like a dentist telling you he must pull a molar instead of an eyetooth. It was hard for us to spare anything.

He went right to work and in the early afternoon, the job was finished. We still had about a hundred miles ahead of us. Failure to arrive at Kankakee before the hospital offices closed would mean we would have to remain in town overnight and arrange for Maude's release the next day. That would be next to impossible. We had no money for even the cheapest kind of a hotel room.

In spite of urging "Leaping" along at a good pace, the clock showed five-fifteen when we drove up in front of the institution's administration building in Kankakee. The doors were not locked yet, but doctors and office workers were leaving. We headed for Dr. Morrow's office and learned that he had gone home.

There was a social worker standing by a desk, gathering her purse and gloves and shoving papers into a drawer. She asked, "What do you want?" We told her that we had come to take a patient out.

"You will have to come back tomorrow for that", she told us. We excitedly blurted that we couldn't. We couldn't come tomorrow. She paused. We thought she was going to ask why, but she didn't. Instead she asked, "Do you have a letter?"

We quickly thrust Dr. Morrow's letter into her hand.

She read. "Maude Oberg! Is that the patient? I know this case. Maude doesn't have a relative to take her. She has no home to go to. How come they are releasing her to you? Where did you meet Maude Oberg?"

My answer was a little slow in coming, but I managed to say, "In here."

"You worked here then?" she asked.

This time my reply got stuck in my throat, and so she asked again, "You worked here on the office staff or as a social worker, perhaps?"

I realized the effect my answer was going to have, but I had to tell the truth.

"I met Maude Oberg when I was an alcoholic patient in here."

"You—a patient!" she exclaimed shrilly. "They are releasing Maude Oberg to an *ex-patient*? Is that what you are telling me?"

I motioned to the letter she was holding in her hand. It was all I could do, for my voice was gone.

"But this—this—" she stammered, waving the letter with a shrug. "This means nothing. There has been a mistake—that's all." Her eyes narrowed to a squint. She was scrutinizing not just our faces, but our clothes. We felt self-conscious and awkward. A frayed coat sleeve and a faded blouse shouted poverty.

Her tone lowered. "Do you know that, in the history of this institution or any other, they have *never* released a drug addict to an alcoholic patient? They just don't do that."

We stood looking at her. We heard then what we thought were her final words: "There has been a terrible mistake—a misunderstanding." With this, she turned and left.

Our knees were week—mine were shaking. We sank down on a little bench there in the hall and looked at each other for encouragement. Each saw only bafflement and confusion in the face of the other. There seemed to be nothing to do—nothing to say. Then both of us bowed our heads and prayed, "This is Your plan, Lord. Maude Oberg needs Your help. We don't know how we can get her out of here, but we know You can do it. Amen."

When we raised our heads, we saw the social worker approaching. Her tone was different. "Yes," she said, "the release is official. There has been no mistake. I can't understand it. Will you come with me?"

She took us into one of the doctor's offices. He was not one that I knew or had met, but few doctors were left in the building at this hour. Papers were scattered all over his desk. He looked up long enough to ask, "You don't drink anymore?" He dropped his eyes back to the pile of papers as I answered, telling him how the Lord had delivered Clara and me from this habit.

"What kind of work do you do?"

I told him. He turned to the social worker. "See if Dr. Weaver is still in the building. Her signature should be on this."

The social worker rushed out and was soon back. "Yes, but they must come right away. Dr. Weaver is leaving now."

The doctor handed us the papers he had been studying and said, "Dr. Weaver will sign these. Then you can go right over to the 8-North Ward and get Maude Oberg. I'll telephone the ward and tell them to have her ready to go."

"Thank you," we said, and rushed in the direction he had pointed.

As we neared Dr. Weaver's office, I remembered when she had me transferred to Ward 8-North for asking for ten dollars from my trust fund to buy cigarettes. It was known that she had no sympathy for alcoholics. I looked forward to this fast-approaching moment when I would be able to tell her that now, through the Lord, I had won complete victory over the cigarette habit as well as drinking. She should be pleased I thought. When we reached her office, the door was open. We saw her sitting at her desk searching through a clutter of papers, much annoyed.

"Dr. Weaver—" I began. She waved her hand and without looking up said, "Hurry, give me those papers."

I walked to her desk and handed them to her, saying again, "Dr. Weaver, I—"

"Here, you sign these." She pushed three or four sheets my way. Her eyes still upon her desk, she scrawled her name on a number of papers, then pushed some more over for me to sign. She had not looked up yet. My name had meant nothing. If she read my signature, it was evident that she had not remembered me.

I wanted to say, "Dr. Weaver, remember me? I'm Jane Page. I was once on your ward as an alcoholic patient. You had me transferred to 8-North, remember?"

But Dr. Weaver was anxious to leave, and after giving me one set of papers and shoving the rest in her drawer, she snapped, "All right now. Go on. I'm in a hurry. I've got to leave."

I was very disappointed. I had so wanted to refresh Dr. Weaver's memory, but she had not given me the least opening. She had not even once looked into my face.

(Later, when we got outside and headed "Leaping" toward 8-North, I thought that perhaps God had a reason for all this, especially the peculiar incident of Dr. Weaver's failure to look at me. Had she done so—well, who knows? God knows how to arrange things, and so I accepted this, too, as part of His plan.)

Maude's face was wreathed in smiles as we drove up in front of 8-North. Her little bundle of clothing was under her arm as she waited at the door. Loudly and excitedly, she was bidding everyone goodbye, kissing patients and attendants and promising to write. When she climbed into "Leaping," she leaned out the window waving and calling up to patients whose voices could be heard from the windows. Some had even climbed up the bars, banging tin cups, screaming; some were cheering, others crying. Voices mingled, but many called after her, "Don't forget us, Maude."

Ten minutes earlier, Maude had been sitting playing cards with two other patients. When the ward phone rang, they teased, "That's for you, Maude." It was a tired, old, humorless joke; no one ever called or visited Maude Oberg. But these patients were not being deliberately cruel: they just lacked sensitivity. And Maude had developed a callus to protect her from such hurts. The attendant turned from the phone and loudly called, "Maude Oberg, it *is* for you. Get your things together, they're coming to take you out."

Maude felt a tingling sensation through her body. What? Had she heard right? Would anyone be so cruel as to joke like this?

The attendant was serious. "Go on, Maude. Don't just sit there staring!"

Maude sputtered, "But—but—but who?" Still incredulous, she gathered and wrapped her things and stood waiting, looking out the window.

The attendant and the other patients shared her excitement and suspense. Who could be coming to take her out, they all wondered.

When she saw an old, battered Ford drive up, she did not associate it as a thing that would have meaning in her life. Even in her anxious and excited moment, she could laugh, and laugh she did—at that ridiculously funny beat-up old wreck.

Then, lo! Jane and Clara were getting out of it, and they were coming up the walk. It couldn't be true—it couldn't! They could not be the ones who were taking her out! These were the least likely people in all the world to be able to do this.

She remembered a year ago, when upon Jane's own release, Jane had promised to come back and get her. How Jane had worried about Maude pinning her hopes on this promise! She needn't have. Maude had never thought for a moment that such a thing could be done.

And now, as she saw Jane and Clara coming up the walk toward the door, she still found it hard to believe. Was this really happening, or would she wake up and find it was all a dream?

Chapter Seventeen

In the car—the car whose appearance had made her laugh—Maude sat happily. She was excited as they drove out through the great iron gates. In a matter of minutes they had arrived in the city of Kankakee, where Jane pulled the car over to the curb.

"What now?" Maude wondered. "Are they going to switch cars? Perhaps they're going to ditch this old wreck here."

But Clara said, "Let us all bow our heads and thank the Lord for what He has done this day."

Sitting in the back seat, Maude slid down so that people passing couldn't see her. She was ashamed to be sitting in this car with the two women up front bowing their heads and praying. *Praying*, out on the street in broad daylight! What would people think? She was genuinely embarrassed. "Besides," she thought, "they are carrying this a little too far. I know they put on a religious act to impress the doctors, but I'm out of there now. They don't have to pretend any longer." She decided to wait and let the girls break the news of their racket and tell her everything in their own time. "I won't ask questions. I'll wait until they are ready to talk."

Conversation fell into natural courses. Maude talked of how glad she was to be out. She described when, the week before, she was called before a staff of doctors who questioned her. She thought this must be routine procedure. It was the first time, however, she had appeared before authorities since she had been in the institution.

She commented on how glad she was that Dr. Weaver had not been there. She was sure Dr. Weaver did not like her. But in all this conversation, Maude was hoping that the girls would soon break and tell her what everything was all about.

When they had driven about fifty miles, Maude began to feel that they were delaying unnecessarily. When were they going to ditch this ridiculous car and get into a Buick or Cadillac and be on their way? How long were they going to keep her waiting before they told her about their new racket?

She was somewhat disgusted. "I've been in that place eighteen months," she brooded. "They ought to know I need a drink. When are they going to pass the bottle?"

Just as the thought completed itself, Clara and Jane burst out in song—"And He walks with me, and He talks with me, and He tells me I am His own."

Maude was stunned. An old hymn she had heard years ago in church when she was a child. Why were they singing that? What was this all about, anyway?

She sat back quietly to figure it out. Well, after all, these women had known each other a long time. Neither of them knew her too well. Before they confided their new racket, before they took her into the gang, they were no doubt "putting the feelers in," seeing how she would react under all circumstances. Maude settled back in her seat smugly. "Pretty smart they are! Well, they won't be disappointed in me. I'll play right along with them. I'll show them I'm smart, too."

But she did notice a difference in their appearance. The shabby clothes, like the old car, were no doubt part of the act, but their faces were different. Clara had always had one or two black eyes whenever she had visited Jane in the state hospital. She had no black eyes now, and neither Clara nor Jane wore makeup. That was unusual. But again, that could be part of the religious pose to impress the doctors.

But their language—they weren't swearing. Neither one had cursed in all this time. And come to think of it, neither of them had smoked a cigarette. Maude knew Jane was a chain-smoker. Strange—this was all mighty strange! Well, *she* would smoke; she had been smoking ever since she got into the car, and she had a good-sized wad of tobacco in her cheek, too.

They talked some more. They talked about Kankakee, the patients, the attendants and the food. Finally, conversation dwindled. It was late at night now. They were on the outskirts of Detroit.

"Well, they had the gall to drive this wreck of a car all the way in. Why? What gives? What is their racket and when are they going to let me in on it?" Maude wondered.

Maude closed her eyes for a while. She was tired. All

this was a little too much for her. Then she heard Jane whisper to Clara, "Shall we take Henry to the alley?"

"Of course—of course! Now it's coming. They're planning to take someone by the name of Henry to the alley—to rob him, no doubt."

She listened. There was no audible reply, but approaching headlights let Maude glimpse Clara's head nodding yes. "Pretty raw stunt," Maude thought. They were going right into action—rob somebody, with her along, and not even let her in on the plans. She didn't like this way of doing things. But after all, they had taken her out of Kankakee, and the least she could do was to go along until she learned what everything was all about.

Now the car was in city traffic. Maude, still silent in the back seat, thought it best to pretend to be asleep. She heard Clara say, "Here's Henry now." Maude thought, "Ah, any moment now, the robbery's coming off!"

Then she heard Jane answer, "Thank you, Clara."

Clara's voice was saying, "You almost missed the street. You must remember, if you want to park the car in the alley, you must turn down Henry Street. Otherwise, you will find yourself on Cass Avenue and then you will have to park in front. There isn't always space there, you know."

Maude's face turned red—very, very red.

Climbing the stairs, she wondered, "Will this act be carried over to the apartment, too? No, it couldn't be. However rough-looking on the outside, they probably have it quite ritzy inside." It was in the wee hours of the morning when they ushered her into a tiny room with a frail-looking wire bed, one chair and an orange crate. They pulled the curtain closed and whispered, "Good night, Maude dear."

The ridiculous touch was the elaborate box of bath salts sitting proudly atop the orange crate. Maude felt like crying, but she laughed. Then she laid her head down on the pillow and laughed some more—then she cried. "What have I gotten into?" was her last conscious thought before she drifted off to sleep.

The following day, Maude saw the room where Clara and Jane slept. Its only window faced a brick wall. Its furnishings were simple—one double bed, two chairs, a dresser and a table. They did their cooking on the two-burner gas jet. Jane painted her signs on the table. They also did their laundry in that room.

Maude said to herself, "If they *are* in a racket, it's a rotten one. It's not paying off and I don't want to get in it."

During the next few days, Maude experienced something akin to the "heat-freeze" treatment employed in tempering metals. One minute she would think, "Now they're warming up. I'm about to find out the meaning of all this." Then, the very next minute, her expectations would take a cold plunge, as Jane suggested, "Let us read a Psalm before breakfast," or Clara would say, "Shall we bow our heads and give thanks for our food?" Their frequent exclamations of "Praise the Lord!" were more than puzzling—they were annoying.

It was now evident to Maude that Clara and Jane were not in a racket, as she had supposed, but that they were *really* very poor, and genuinely sincere in their joy and religious fervor. There could be only one answer to the riddle of their sudden change of character: both of these young women—these poor unfortunate women—had lost their minds.

After the second day of Psalm reading, prayers before breakfast, dinner and supper, with injections of praise in every conversation, Maude sat on the frail bed behind her curtained doorway and cried. She had not indulged in self-pity too often. She had always taken punishment realizing that she had it coming. She had taken kicks and abuses planning to kick back.

In the past, alcohol or drugs seemed to take away the sharp edge from her sufferings, but Maude completely broke down and felt very very sorry for herself. She was no kid. It was high time to settle down in some well-planned, good paying racket with not too much risk, and live with a view to the future.

But look what had happened to her! She spoke her thoughts aloud—"Here I just got out of the nuthouse, and now I'm living with two of them!"

What was she to do? With each sob, the rusty bedsprings creaked. She wondered, "It is strange. They're both off—both of them went crazy on the same thing—religion!" She cried some more, and every slight body movement sounded off the mournful accompaniment of the bedsprings. She would have to stop crying and think—think hard. There must be a way out. If she just ran off and left these girls, where would she go? And besides, the poor things were awfully nice. Running away from them now would be a cruel thing to do. They meant well and they were sharing the little they had, and were so happy about doing it. She began to feel truly sorry for those poor, poor girls. In this poverty, and with their minds gone!

With sympathy in her heart for the two women, she decided she must not leave them now. Later she would, of course. But she would stay for a week or so, and she would get along with them, too. Maude knew how to do that. She had learned in the state hospital that the best way to get along with demented people is to humor them. Well, she knew what to do to humor these girls.

Next Sunday would be Easter. Being crazy on religion, they would naturally want to go to church. All right! She would surprise them. She would suggest it herself. That would make them happy. Crazy or not, Maude found that she was liking them. "They are good to me and they are already calling me 'Mother'."

Maude, Clara, and Jane

Chapter Eighteen

When Easter Sunday morning came, Maude appeared in our room highly rouged and painted, her hair fuzzed; she was glittering with dimestore finery.

"I'm ready to go to church," she chirped.

We were surprised.

When we were alone, Clara remarked, "Isn't this wonderful? Already she wants to know about God." I was happy, too, but I thought it might be wise to hint to Maude that she was overdressed. "That would be the worst thing we could do!" Clara objected.

As we entered the church, people nodded and greeted us pleasantly and heartily, including Maude. We could not help noticing many startled eyes.

"Clara," I whispered, "we should have told her. She will be embarrassed."

Clara winked. "Don't worry, kid. It's turning out all

right. Look at Maude's face."

I looked. Maude was beaming. It was evident that she noticed the wide eyes and decided that they were staring in admiration.

When the congregation rose to sing, Maude's voice boomed rich and vibrant, way above the voices of hundreds—"Up from the grave He arose—!" The song leader indicated to hold that last note. And Maude held it. Heads turned. Everyone looked her way. This time, the looks *were* truly of admiration.

"She has a magnificent voice," I thought. It stirred me. It stirred others. I looked at Clara. She was wiping tears from her cheeks. "I didn't know she could sing like that!" I had told Clara, but I fell short in describing Maude's voice. Now she heard and was thrilled. Everyone was thrilled and blessed as Maude's voice soared above that great congregation. It was more than a strong, loud voice—it was melodic, it was rich and deep—it was lovely!

That afternoon, we listened as Maude told us something of her torturous addictions of the past. She had used alcohol, then switched to narcotics. She had been a chef, she said, which is what they call one who prepared opium for smoking. She had sniffed cocaine, smoked marijuana, used morphine, and was a "mainliner." The habit was costly, and she finally had to peddle dope to get enough money for her own supply. When she could not get the stuff, she had tried to break the habit in psychopathic wards. Whenever they arrested her for some charge or other, she had to break "cold turkey"—without sedation or any medication at all.

In such times of torment, she broke windows and ate chips of glass. The gnawing in her stomach caused her to swallow open safety pins, hoping she would die. She was near death many times, and once was even pronounced dead. Somehow, she lived through all of this.

As she described these torments, I could well remember my own agony as I lay suffering delirium tremens, screaming in anguish, feeling myself sucked into a tunnel of darkness. I had lain with wild bulging eyes, spittle foaming from parched lips, the cords of my neck drawn tight, my breath coming in convulsions; my wrists pinned to the bedside, shackled, and my ankles shackled, too, so I wouldn't bash my head against the wall in madness.

Gruesome and terrifying it was. I sighed, "God has taken us out of all that. He has delivered us! Let us thank Him!"

Right there, we bowed our heads in gratitude to the Lord. Maude was silent. We could not read her thoughts, but we were certain Maude was thinking very seriously.

That evening, knowing Maude's love for music, we took her to another church where they had an Easter cantata. She was thrilled through every minute of it. At the conclusion, the minister gave a very short message and invited sinners to accept Christ. He asked for hands to be raised. Maude looked around. She saw hands go up, so she lifted hers. When we saw her hand, we were very elated.

An earnest little woman rushed to Maude's side and grabbed her elbow. "Come, dear," she said, "come down to the altar."

Maude, disengaging her elbow somewhat roughly, asked, "What for?"

"To be saved," the woman said insistently and grabbed Maude's elbow again.

Aggravated, Maude turned to me. Her voice was not too soft and everyone around could hear, "What is this? They ask people to raise their hands, and now they try to rush business. What kind of place is this?"

Maude was angry.

I said to the woman, "I appreciate your concern. She doesn't know what it's all about, but she is seeking." The earnest little woman retreated. I looked at Maude and saw that she had quieted down. In the car as we drove home, I heard Maude repeating to herself the words "seeking—seeking—seeking."

That night, Maude went to her room and prayed the first real prayer she had ever prayed in her life. "Dear God, Jane told that woman I am 'seeking.' Yes, I've been seeking something all my life, but what am I seeking? I never believed in You, but Clara and Jane think You are real, and they are better off than I am. I'm no good. I can't stay with these girls, because I'm no good. I'm just asking You one thing, God. Don't let me be a hindrance to these girls. Don't let me hurt them. Rather than let me stand in their way or spoil their faith, send me—send me back to the nuthouse. Amen."

Maude's pillow was wet with tears that night.

Shortly after Maude's arrival, Maude, Clara and I were sitting in our little room thinking about what we would have for our evening meal. Clara suggested Spanish rice, and that met with the approval of all. There were other things we liked better, but they would not fit our budget.

A knock came on the door, and when we opened it, there stood Ray, our neighbor from the room up front. He was smiling and had in his hand a large can of a famous brand coffee. It could be truly said that if the three of us lusted for anything, it was for good coffee. We were using cheap grades and we were dissatisfied. And Maude, although she did not complain, found our beverage almost nauseating. Clara and I were glad for this gift, but Maude was radiant. She grabbed the can out of Ray's hand and hugged it to her bosom. "Real coffee! We have real coffee!"

While I was busy thanking Ray, he was talking at the same time about how he and Ada always wished to do some little thing to show appreciation. I was not paying too much attention to what he was saying until I heard: "Well, I saw my chance. I was alone in that corner of the supermarket and no one was looking, so I just snatched a couple of cans. I figured, one for you folks and one for us!"

I was looking at Ray with my mouth wide open, but he hadn't noticed. "Well, enjoy it, girls!" he said, as he closed the door after him.

Maude danced around in circles, still hugging the coffee. I fell silent. Clara busied herself in preparation of the evening meal. Finally, Maude noticed the change of mood and frowned. "What's the matter?"

I opened my mouth to say, "Oh, nothing." But no sound came out. The Lord had instantly convicted me that would have been a lie. "Well, come on!" Maude prodded. "Tell me, what is the matter?"

Clara was not looking my way. She was deeply engrossed with her cooking. I straightened my shoulders and began, "Well, this will be hard for you to understand, Maude."

That is as far as I got. Fear settled over me. Here we were trying to win Maude Oberg to the Lord—to a new way of life—and all we had shown her so far was poverty. We had invited her to come with us to share "our nothing." She was certainly being a good sport about it, but now that this gift of coffee had made her happy, how could I tell her that we must give it back to Ray?

I stood there looking dumb. Maude's features relaxed. She said calmly, "Don't be afraid, Jane. Tell me what is wrong."

I was fumbling with my explanation. Clara, trying to clarify things, fumbled along with me. "You see, if we didn't know—well, Ray shouldn't have stolen that coffee and if he hadn't told us—" Maude smiled. It was a sweet, patient smile.

She said, "All right girls, I understand."

She thrust the coffee into my hands.

"Give it to Ray," she said simply.

I started to stammer a further explanation. "Don't you think that I know you have no choice but to return that coffee?" Maude interrupted. "Were you to keep it, you would be sharing in the theft, really. Believing as you do, you couldn't be party to anyone's theft."

Nodding and backing out the door, and grateful to the Lord for Maude's understanding at a time when my courage faltered, I hurried next door and returned the coffee to Ray.

I seemed to have gathered strength, for I did not falter as I told Ray our reasons for being unable to accept his gift. Ray was not offended, but he was embarrassed. And we since prayed that he would be convicted in his soul, for conviction of sin leads to repentance.

One of the nearby churches was having revival services. The Cleveland Colored Quintette was singing, and Bonna Flemming was preaching. Maude willingly went with us to these meetings. The first night, she squirmed uneasily in her seat. She told us afterwards that for a time she thought we had told the evangelist all about her. Everything he said seemed to hit. Then, suddenly, she realized that her own conscience had applied the message to her life. She had a second session of prayer that night in her room.

"Dear Lord, I don't want to go back to the old life. I am beginning to like—well, I like—I love—these girls, and they love me. They call me Mother. Show me what to do. They're Christians and I'm not. I can't stay with them because I'm not like they are. Do you suppose, God, I could ever be like them?"

The next night, the Quintette sang songs of joy and blessing, and the evangelist preached a powerful message. When he finished, he asked those who wanted to accept Christ to come forward and kneel at the altar. Clara and I were sitting with our heads bowed, praying, but peeking every once in a while through our fingers to watch Maude. Both of us knew when Maude left her seat and went forward. We were beside ourselves with joy. We didn't go up with her, but let God meet her there. We felt clumsy, inadequate. We feared to thrust ourselves, or anything we could do or say, into Maude's solemn moment of decision.

When Maude came back from the altar, we looked at her and we knew! Yes, we knew. We knew! Maude Oberg was saved!

"Tell us how it happened. Oh Maude, tell us about it," we joyously urged.

Maude said, "Well, I knew I had come to the crossroads. I knew I didn't want to go back to the old life, but if I left you girls, that is what would happen. I dreaded and feared it. I knew you two had something wonderful—something that I needed—and now I wanted it, too. When I went forward to the altar, I knelt there, not knowing how to pray. People came and knelt around me. They were praying and crying. I listened and heard them praying for ME. They were crying out to God for my soul. How could people who had never met me love me like that? I wondered. How could they care enough about me to cry like that and to pray? Then I wondered how you girls could want a woman old enough to be your mother, who knew nothing but crime and imprisonment all her life—a murderer and a criminal. What could cause you to love me enough to do what you did, to take me into your home and share with me the little you had?

"Then I knew. Suddenly, I knew. Nothing but the love of Christ in the hearts of those people could cause them to cry and pray like that for me. And nothing but the love of Christ in your hearts could cause you to take me with you. I knew exactly what to do then. I prayed. I said, 'Dear Lord, I want what these people have, what these girls have. I ask You to forgive my sins, Lord Jesus, and to come into my heart and save my soul'."

Maude's tear-bright eyes were smiling. She added, "And I meant it."

Chapter Nineteen

After Maude Oberg's conversion, the three of us lived together in Detroit as a family for the next five years. During that time, we were able to have my father with us for a visit and I had the wonderful privilege of leading him to the Lord. He died about a year later.

My little sign business prospered somewhat, and we were able to rent a four-room furnished apartment in a better neighborhood. Clara worked as a waitress until, because of a physical ailment, her doctor advised against standing on her feet for long hours. She had to quit this type of work, but the Lord opened a job for me as an artist for one of the large automobile manufacturers.

Maude, at our insistence, stayed in the home and kept house as a mother. Her joy was boundless. She looked so very different from the Maude Oberg we had met in the Kankakee State Hospital. Her hair was not clipped short now, but grew into an abundant crop of wavy folds which Maude piled high upon her head. Its red-gold sheen framed a very lovely face that smiled in radiant joy. Every line of the cheek and crease of the brow was a furrow of the plowing of the soul that God made fruitful. And every onlooker could see, in Maude's features, the gnarled beauty—as a tree that had been bent in strong winds of adversity, in whose rough exterior bark is the touch of majesty. She had been through the storms of life, and she knew! She knew the terror and pain of battering winds that had cast her down, down to the foot of the cross of Christ, where she had repented and was made new. All this was etched in Maude's countenance. People were drawn to her, not knowing exactly why. They knew only that there was something mysteriously wonderful about this woman. And they heard from her what this "something wonderful" was.

The milkman, the butcher, the grocer and just everyone heard what the Lord had done for her—for us all. Because of God's victory in our lives, we were able to help other patients out of the Kankakee State Hospital where Maude and I were once inmates. One by one, we took some of these women to live with us in our small apartment and shared with them until they got jobs and had means to support themselves elsewhere. Always, we pleaded with them to accept Christ and to know the joy and peace that now possessed our own hearts. Some of them did, but we did not cease to help those who refused. We continued to show God's love. Soon, we were testifying in the local hospitals, jails and missions. Churches of all denominations asked for our testimonies, too.

In 1946, God called me to give up my job. We left our cozy apartment. He sent us forth throughout these United

States and into parts of Canada to tell of His redeeming power in our lives. We spoke with gratitude and joy, and rejoiced to see many lives influenced for Christ through our message. It was as we traveled about as prison missionaries that we became aware of the need for women's rescue work. We noticed there were, in most of the large cities, missions for men, but women's needs were overlooked somehow—tragically neglected. We prayed to be used of God in helping women chained in darkness as we once were.

In 1951, we opened the Home of the Ministering Friends in Miami, Florida—our first rescue home for friendless women. In 1954, we opened our second rescue home in Brooklyn, New York. In these homes, we received and helped women released from jails and state hospitals; women off the streets, women stranded, in trouble and distress. We told them of a God who is able to deliver from all sin and offered our own testimonies as evidence. We made no charge for this help. The homes were supported through the free-will giving of God's people who desired to help us help others.

Through the years, the Lord greatly blessed the ministry of these homes. Maude Oberg and Clara De Runtz managed the home in Miami, and Esther Walsh, a consecrated registered nurse, devoted her life full time as co-director with me of the home in Brooklyn. It turned out that Esther remained with me as my dear companion, co-worker and friend for nearly forty years.

Why have I told this story? Surely I have not told it to boast of a sinful and sordid past—nor in pride of accomplishment. "Not that we are sufficient of ourselves to think any thing as of ourselves; but our sufficiency is of God" (II

Cor. 3:5). Then, why have I told this story? Because I've been forgiven much to love much. And I love you enough to share my "love story" with you. A stranger? No! You are either a sinner lost or a sinner saved—just like I WAS, or just like I AM. You are no stranger to me.

Nor should you consider me a stranger to you. No matter how awful you think my sins are, and how assured you are that you've never committed such offenses, the truth of the matter is, we have both sinned and both need the merciful forgiveness of God. The Savior did not suffer on the cross because of our overt acts of sin—for they were only symptoms of the sin in our desperately wicked, unregenerated hearts—our carnal nature with which we were born. That's why Jesus said, "You must be born again" (John 3:7).

Esther Walsh

Part I has clearly shown God's wonderful love for poor lost sinners such as I. Since I have titled my autobiography *Forgiven Much—to Love Much*, I am sure I made clear that God truly loves very much indeed, for He forgives much. Yes, very much! For He forgives ALL sins of each repentant soul. And now, to be true to my theme, I must show the result (consequence, fruit) of the love and forgiveness the Lord bestowed on me. I have shown the Lord's "much love," and now I must show mine.

Is it time for me to brag—to list what I might consider my good deeds? I think not! But then, why not? Because, dear readers, I don't know what they are. I've written about the lives of Maude, Clara, and myself after our conversions; how we lived together and worked together serving the Lord. To tell all would require another book or two, but limited time restricts me. I am already on borrowed time, having far exceeded the allotted "threescore and ten years." I am offering but a sketch.

As you read, you will see God's transforming power at work, for which He is to receive all the glory. But as for our part—as for ME particularly, I will say with Paul, "I judge not mine own self" (I Cor. 4:3)—I have not attained, but am pressing on toward, the high calling. God's Word tells us not to think of ourselves more highly than we ought. That doesn't mean, of course, that we will lack awareness of the righteousness and grace the Lord has wrought within us. We will hear His "well done" along life's road, as well as at the end of it.

The story of my life is told in a factual manner. I've simply told what happened without embellishment.

When reporting my conversion experience, I described events as they were. It matters not whether I understood them or liked them then or even now—I told what happened. The atmosphere in this revival service was new and strange to me. You've read the description in Chapter 9. People shouted, waved their arms in the air, some jumped, some swooned. Somehow I was not overtaken by confusion, although there probably were some rabid fanatics in that crowd. Even so, the crowd as a whole radiated love and true joy, and that's what I saw and felt. It was in that atmosphere that I was saved. I realize the same atmosphere repulsed my friend Clara, and had I not been "ripe" for salvation, I might have turned away, too. But the Lord was showing me things, and no fog could obliterate what God wanted me to see. I saw love and joy and blessing!

I can't, of course, vouch that everyone in that crowded tent was a true believer in Christ, but those who were radiated Christ's love to me—waving, shouting, jumping, not withstanding. And God's love was born in my heart then and still lives in my heart now—for my blessed Lord and for ALL His people. I love to love. You see, I've been forgiven much to love much.

Your
Ministering
Friend,

Jane Page

Holy!, Holy!, is what the angels sing,
And I intend to help them
Make the Courts of Heaven ring!

But when I tell salvation's story
They shall fold their wings,

For angels never knew the joy
That my salvation brings!

—J. OATMAN, JR. (1894)—